ACE COLLINS

SERVICE TAILS

MORE STORIES
★ ★ ★
OF MAN'S BEST HERO

Guideposts
New York

SERVICE TAILS
MORE STORIES OF MAN'S BEST HERO

Published by Guideposts Books & Inspirational Media

39 Old Ridgebury Road, Suite 27
Danbury, CT 06810
Guideposts.org

This Guideposts edition has been published by special arrangement with Abingdon Press.

Library of Congress Cataloging-in-Publication Data

Names: Collins, Ace, author.
Title: Service tails : more stories of man's best hero / Ace Collins.
Description: First [edition]. | Nashville,Tennessee : Abingdon Press, 2016.
Identifiers: LCCN 2016009314 | ISBN 9781501820076 (pbk.)
Subjects: LCSH: Service dogs—United States—Anecdotes. | Animal heroes—
    United States—Anecdotes.
Classification: LCC HV1569.6 .C65 2016 | DDC 362.4/048—dc23 LC record available at
https://lccn.loc.gov/2016009314

Scripture quotation from The Authorized (King James) Version. Rights in the Authorized Version in the United Kingdom are vested in the Crown. Reproduced by permission of the Crown's patentee, Cambridge University Press.

The persons and events portrayed in this work of fiction are the creations of the author, and any resemblance to persons living or dead is purely coincidental.

This Guideposts edition was typeset by Aptara, Inc.

Printed and bound in the United States of America

10 9 8 7 6 5 4 3 2 1

CONTENTS

Introduction v

Beginnings 1

Finding Love 23

Team Potential 39

Memories 55

Employing Experience 71

Down but Not Out 85

A Ticket to Ride 103

Maintaining Balance 121

Hope 137

Ignoring Barriers 155

Unconditional 173

Service Forgotten 187

Further Stories of Dedicated Dogs 201

Introduction

This is not a book that spotlights heroic dogs wildly tossing themselves into lifesaving situations. Yes, some of the dogs in this book have saved lives, but their purpose is service. In just doing their jobs, each of these dogs stretches the way we see both canine and human potential. As they lead the way to independence for people whose disabilities were supposed to limit their lives, these dogs open our eyes and our minds. Their training was intense, their loyalty unquestioned, and each step of the way, they constantly adapt to better serve those they lead. They are more than heroes; they are servants.

From a Swiss German shepherd that came to the United States in the late 1920s to initiate a movement that would touch and impact millions of lives and change the very perception of a nation's view on disabilities, to a collie that began life as a mobility animal and grew into a woman's guide through Alzheimer's disease, from a big Lab that led a blind woman through college and guided her into marriage, to a golden retriever mix that opened the door to life for a child locked in a world of solitude and misunderstanding, these chapters introduce us to leaders whose entire lives are wrapped in the banner of service. The stories are remarkable snapshots of the value of teamwork and imagination as well as devotion to duty and unconditional love and acceptance.

Except for the initial chapter that presents the story of the canine and young man who started the service dog movement, all of the stories in this book are contemporary. Those served range from a middle school student to a woman in her nineties. While each person's need is unique, all are tied together by a canine's ability to free them of the limits placed on their lives, not just by disabilities or circumstances, but by a society's misconceptions. These are, therefore, people who live in our world and serve as role models and inspiration. Their stories will open our eyes and minds to the unrealized rewards of teamwork.

I could not have written this book without the help and support of Katie Malatino of Canine Companions for Independence, Karen Woon of Guide Dogs for the

Blind, and Leslie Rappaport of Kings Valley Collies. I highly recommend their organizations. The links to the sites are listed below. I also need to thank Michael Hingson and Debbie Abbenante.

In closing I am reminded of the familiar African proverb "It takes a village." After conducting the interviews and doing the research for this book, I would like to suggest a new proverb, "It takes a dog." Once you read these unique "tails," you will likely agree that a dog can literally take us anywhere.

www.cci.org
www.guidedogs.com
www.kingsvalleycollies.com/mobility

Beginnings

Coming together is a beginning; keeping together is a progress; working together is success.

Henry Ford

Sometimes leading also means following. Sometimes being first means you actually arrive second.

A movement began with an athletic young man from Tennessee.

Morris Frank was fortunate to be born into a wealthy family in Nashville. In fact, if his family had not had money, his life and the lives of hundreds of thousands of others with disabilities might have been far different and much less productive. In this case, money was anything but the root of all evil. Rather, it was the launching pad for a revolution.

In 1914, when he was just six, Morris lost the sight in his right eye when he was struck by a tree limb while horseback riding. Coincidentally, his mother had lost her sight in the same fashion. During a boxing match a decade later, the teen lost vision in his left eye. Suddenly, just like his mom, he was completely blind.

In the early 1920s, there were few options for disabled people. Most were not educated and had to depend upon their families for everything. Morris was the exception. Because of his family's wealth, the boy had opportunities that even those without visual impairments rarely received. His father hired readers so his son could attend an outstanding prep academy. With the help of paid human guides, Morris continued to go to exclusive summer camps in Maine and freely travel in both Nashville and up and down the East Coast. Even the doors to Vanderbilt University swung open for the young man when he graduated from high school.

Outgoing, charming, and driven, Morris thrived. By twenty he was a top-notch student and a successful insurance salesman. He was a regular at the local social scene and had a large group of friends who gladly offered rides to Nashville's premier events. It seemed the only things the well-dressed young man lacked were dependable employees. Those hired to read his lessons and review his insurance policies, as well as drive him to school and appointments, often didn't show up on time. Sometimes they didn't show up at all. Thus, in the one area where he really needed independence, he had none.

When his human guides didn't show up, Morris was forced to use a cane. The modern world's urban challenges were at times overwhelming. His outings with the only tool available for the blind took much longer than those using a human guide. Thus, he was often late for appointments, meetings, and school. The screech of tires became a common sound as he crossed a street unaware that a car or truck was in his path. Once, a wrong turn and a misstep caused him to tumble almost twenty feet into a freshly dug trench. Not able to climb out, he had to wait hours until a passerby discovered his predicament and helped him. In time he began to understand why most blind people stayed home.

It was a frustrated Morris who, in the late fall of 1927, sat in the family's living room listening to his father read from a recent issue of *The Saturday Evening Post*. John Frank's evening readings had been a tradition in the family since his wife, Jessie, had gone blind. For the past four years, Morris had also come to depend upon his father and these nightly gatherings to keep abreast of world events.

On that cool night, John read a story written by
Dorothy Harrison Eustis called "The Seeing Eye." In
the article, Eustis wrote about German shepherd dogs
being trained in Europe to lead soldiers blinded in
The Great War (now known as World War I). Morris
intently listened, growing more and more excited as he
pictured the way these dogs had brought men independence and value. The concept of a dog being the eyes
for a blind man was almost inconceivable. How could
the dog know when to stop and go? How could he
determine the proper routes to take and how to avoid
danger? This had to be a piece of fiction. There was no
way that in one little corner of the world the blind were
no longer dependent on others, that they were working
and traveling on their own.

When his father finished reading, Morris's mind
was whirling. Though he still wondered if this was
nothing more than a fairy tale, a part of the young
man wanted to believe an answer for his problem had
been found.

As a boy, Morris had been his blind mother's guide.
She placed her hand on his shoulder, and he led her
through crowded stores, up steep steps, and across
busy streets. His one good eye had spotted dangers
and pitfalls and helped her avoid them. As he remem-
bered those days, the boy smiled. Maybe a dog

could do those same tasks. Perhaps it wasn't so hard to believe after all.

Morris rose from his chair and walked toward his father. He had to know more, and the only way to do that was to dictate a letter to his father to be sent to the author in care of *The Saturday Evening Post*. In that short introductory correspondence, Morris informed the article's writer of his condition and asked her to verify that the seemingly miraculous story she had woven was completely accurate. If it was really true, he wanted to meet with her. In closing Morris assured Eustis he was willing to travel to the ends of the earth to get a dog that could lead him. The letter was mailed on November 5. Later in life Morris Frank would say that was the moment everything began to change.

For thirty agonizing days the young man waited. Each day he would check the mail, and as time passed, his hopes grew dimmer. He even came to believe the story Eustis had written was likely an exaggeration of the actual facts. The dogs couldn't really do what she had written, and that was the reason she had not answered his letter. By the thirtieth day, Morris had all but given up. He did not even bother going to the post office that early December morning. Thus, he didn't discover that Dorothy Eustis had replied until his father came home from work. In his hands John held an envelope from Fortunate Fields Farms in Switzerland.

Eustis assured Morris that everything she had written was true. In fact, she had only had a chance to cover the basics of the skill sets the dogs had mastered. She then told him of a training center she owned, Fortunate Fields, which educated canines for work with the Red Cross and for various military groups. She then offered an invitation he had hoped for but not expected. If he would be willing to travel from Tennessee to Switzerland, she would bring in a specialized trainer and choose a dog just for Morris. By committing to several weeks of one-on-one work, she believed he would also be able to live out the story she had written for *The Saturday Evening Post*. After dangling the tempting offer, she asked the young man to think about it for a few weeks. She then assured Morris she would call when she visited the United States over the Christmas holidays.

Morris was literally dancing around the family living room. Initially, the family was excited too. Here was a chance for their son to gain a bit more independence. But, after hours of planning everything from what to feed the dog to where it would sleep, reality set in. His mother, Jessie, when considering the young man's solo trip across the Atlantic, began to worry. She had always had great faith in her son, but this was a much different challenge than walking across the Vanderbilt campus. How could he possibly find his way from Nashville to Switzerland? A trip like that would require him to use numerous trains, make a long ocean voyage, spend time in Paris, and then travel to the Alps. He wouldn't know the language or customs. And he would have to deal with several different types of currency. It simply seemed overwhelming. She tried to explain her feelings to Morris, but she quickly discovered the young man was far too fixated on his chance to obtain a dog to listen to reason.

Within days, a long line of friends joined Jessie in trying to convince Morris not to chase this wild dream. Their argument was that a dog was simply not worth the time, expense, and risks associated with the trip. In the long run, the canine would ultimately offer the young man little more than companionship, and any local pup could do that. In visit after visit, they continued to pound home that he was setting himself up for a huge disappointment. Some even thought the young man was falling for a con game.

Morris would later admit he had many of the same concerns. Dogs were great at learning tricks, but leading a blind man would require reasoning skills that most believed had been reserved only for humans. So he, too, wondered how a dog could guide a man through crowded city streets or help him find a specific location. After all, things that sounded too good to be true were usually scams. Was he falling into that trap?

A wavering Morris turned to an expert for advice. Dr. Edward E. Allen, the director of the Perkins Institute for the Blind, was recognized as one of the top experts in the field of vision impairment. If this were just a gimmick, the director would know. Dr. Allen was aware of the German work using dogs and was cautiously optimistic about it. Yet while the man appreciated the concept of a canine replacing a cane, he also wondered about the project's ceiling. Thus, he was not ready to give his full endorsement.

However, Dr. Allen had known Morris for several years. He understood his drive and intelligence. If there was one American who might be able to make this marriage of dog and man work, it was this young man from Tennessee. With that in mind, Dr. Allen encouraged Morris to give it a shot. At the very least it would be an incredible adventure. With this affirmation in his pocket, there was no turning back. When Eustis made her holiday call, the young man enthusiastically told her, "Mrs. Eustis, to get my independence back, I'd go to hell."

Early in the New Year, Morris began the long,

daunting, solitary trip. On the trains that carried him from Nashville to New York, negative viewpoints of the man's condition were easy to spot. People whispered, wondering why a blind man was allowed to travel alone. Others voiced their appreciation to the various train conductors for "taking care of him." In New York, when he boarded the ship, the sense of isolation and gentle ridicule mushroomed. The crew suggested Morris just remain in his cabin so he wouldn't hurt himself or get in the way of the other passengers. They offered to bring him anything he needed if he would just stay out of sight. The independent young man would have none of that. Yet, when he was out on the deck, complete strangers tried to help him walk, find a chair, and order a meal. Even when sharing a postdinner stroll around the ship, Morris could sense their awkwardness. It was as if they viewed him as a toddler. Few took the time to note his wit, intelligence, or charm. He had many of the same interests that they did, but they had no idea what to say to him.

In Paris it was a little different. It was almost as if they resented a disabled person having the gall to venture out in public. No one was interested in directing him to a café or guiding him to the city's historic landmarks. As he waited for connections to take him to Switzerland, he was all but locked in a hotel room.

Therefore the City of Light offered little but darkness for the visiting American.

When he finally stepped off the train in Vevey and felt the cool, crisp Swiss mountain air, everything changed. With Vevey located on a mountainside, Morris could sense the expanse on all sides. The scent of pine trees was everywhere. Unlike New York or Paris, the air was so clean and fresh, it served to reignite his optimism.

Dorothy Eustis greeted him at the station as if he were a long-lost son. As she catered to his needs, she also respected his independence. She directed his movement with her voice rather than trying to lead him with her arm. For the first time in weeks, someone was actually treating him as if he were a fully functioning adult.

Eustis's chalet was large and had a very open feel. The room he would call home for the next few weeks was decorated with antique furniture. His bed was soft, and the sheets finer than any he had ever known. Yet none of this mattered to Morris. His only interest was in meeting his dog and finding out if the canine really could change his life.

After the visitor was settled, Eustis introduced him to Jack Humphrey. Humphrey was an American-born trainer who had been imported to Europe to work for

Eustis's Fortunate Fields Training Center. When he learned of Morris's upcoming visit, he took the time to study the blind and familiarize himself with their specific needs. He then returned to the center and adapted his training methods to dogs that might be able to serve as guides for those who could not see.

During his first few weeks of creating what was literally a new curriculum, Humphrey had even gone so far as to blindfold himself. As he tried to pick his way along roads and city streets with a cane, he became more fully aware of the barriers facing Morris and others who were likewise disabled. That role-playing experience allowed him to better understand the skills a guide dog would need to allow the blind to function independently of human help. As this was something brand-new, trial and error built the model needed to educate both the canine and the human. By the time Morris arrived in Switzerland, Humphrey believed he had a training pattern in hand as well as a dog ready for the task.

Initially Humphrey worked just with Morris. He explained what would be expected of the man and how the marriage of dog and man would work. What was emphasized again and again was the dog would lead the man and the man would have to follow. If the roles were reversed, the experiment would fail.

Only when Morris had a grasp of his role did the
trainer bring a small, dark German shepherd named
Kiss into the room. The initial meeting was not what
Morris expected. The dog showed little interest in him.
Even as they put on the harness and the man grabbed
hold, the dog remained somewhat aloof. Reacting to
Humphrey, she tolerated what she likely viewed as the
very awkward human attempting to give her orders.

Morris would quickly discover that the standoffish
dog was the least of his worries. The visitor's main issues were with the trainer. Humphrey was a hard man
to please. He would not abide commands being issued
in any order but what he prescribed. In fact, the only
time the trainer showed compassion was when Morris
stepped on Kiss's foot. Then Humphrey was worried
only about the dog's well-being.

The roads that the visitor, dog, and trainer walked
each day were slick with snow and ice. The city streets
they traversed were filled with people, cars, trucks,
and horse-drawn carts. In many of the places the team
traveled, they were surrounded by steep drop-offs,
rushing mountain streams, and low-hanging branches.
And all the while Morris was learning to handle the
dog, Humphrey was barking out orders. The young
man heard the critiques so often he wanted to scream.

Always pick up the handle of the harness on left and

keep the dog on your left. You must keep your hand close by your side or you will hit a post or pole. Protect the dog when you sit down. No, not that way. Make sure the dog is completely under the bench or chair so that others won't step on her. And don't pull your dog; she is supposed to pull you. If she stops, you stop because she is trying to tell you something. So listen to her.

Hour after hour and day after day, the orders kept coming. Thanks to often ignoring Humphrey's instructions, the young man ran into trees, poles, and fences and tumbled down a fair share of hillsides. Only after being bruised and battered several times did Morris learn to trust the dog. Then and only then did things get easier.

As Morris grew used to following Kiss's lead, he asked the trainer why the dog often took seemingly erratic routes. Humphrey didn't bother verbally explaining the dog's unique navigation. Rather, he took Morris back to the spots where Kiss had veered off and showed him such things as a low-hanging limb or a sign that the dog could have easily walked under but would have knocked Morris over. When the perplexed visitor asked, "But how did she know how tall I was?" Humphrey explained, "I trained her to know."

One afternoon Morris asked if it would be all right to change the dog's name. Humphrey wanted to know why a change was necessary. Morris answered, "I just don't want to go back home and constantly be calling out for a Kiss. It might just be misunderstood." The trainer laughed and assured Morris he could call the dog anything he wanted. From that point on, the female German shepherd was known as Buddy.

After weeks of hard training, Humphrey announced it was time for solo work. For their first trek, Morris and Buddy would walk down the mountain road to town, do some shopping, and eat a meal. The trainer also suggested the rather shabby American get a haircut. Before the pair left, Humphrey issued a final warning. "Morris, you can be a blind person with a dog or a blind person with eyes. To be the latter, you must trust your dog's eyes." Those words would echo in the man's brain for the rest of this life.

The real partnership between man and dog was born on that trip. Buddy walked the man around poles, kept Morris from being struck by a runaway oxcart, and helped him find a café, the stores he needed, and the barbershop. Hours later when the team returned to the chalet, the young man enthusiastically told Dorothy Eustis, "I'm free. I'm finally free again!"

That night by the fire, Humphrey and Eustis assured their visitor he had passed his tests and it was time for him and Buddy to return home. As he considered all he had learned and what the dog was capable of bringing to his life, Morris quoted Proverbs 20:12, "The hearing ear, and the seeing eye, the LORD hath made even both of them." He then added, "I want to share what you have given me with others. I want the blind in America to have guide dogs. I want to start a school to share this amazing gift."

Eustis laid her hand on the young man's shoulder and gently suggested that for his vision to become a reality, he and Buddy had to first prove themselves. They must show America this wasn't a clever circus stunt. If they could accomplish that, then the woman would help finance a movement to bring guide-dog training to the United States. So the question became, was the young man up to the challenge to prove that this marriage of canine and man could bring independence to the blind?

Morris's return voyage was the first time he fully realized the power of the dog, not just as a guide but also as an icebreaker. With Buddy leading the way, the man quickly moved about the ship. He no longer bumped into anything or anyone, nor did he strike strangers with his cane. But the ease of movement paled in comparison to the reactions of the passengers and crew. People were drawn to Buddy and therefore gave Morris a chance to share his intelligence and humor. Thanks to the dog, Morris was no longer someone to be pitied or shunned. He was an interesting person with a story that folks wanted to know.

Beyond her ability to lead the man around the large ship, Buddy's potential to move beyond her training was displayed when Morris exchanged his French currency for American money. After he left the ship's office and returned to his room, the man panicked. His wallet was not in his coat pocket. A quick search of his empty pants pocket proved that he must have lost it. Without money how was he going to survive in New York City or get back to Nashville? As he sank down on his bed, Buddy leaned forward and dropped the lost wallet into his lap. Amazingly, when Morris had unwittingly dropped the billfold, the dog had picked it up. Thus, Buddy was more than just a well-trained animal; she was capable of making decisions based on observation. She somehow knew that wallet was important, sensed Morris would need it, and, when it had slipped from his pocket, had deemed it something she should retrieve. How she had been able to understand such a seemingly complex issue was just the beginning of her growth as guide, companion, and friend.

Likely because of his Swiss host and his connections to *The Saturday Evening Post*, word of Morris and his remarkable dog had gotten back to the United States. The press was waiting for them at the dock. The unbelieving reporters demanded to see if the German shepherd really could guide the man through New York City streets. Ready or not, it was time to prove Buddy's value.

The dog had been trained in the rural Alps and had never known anything like the Big Apple's congested streets and sidewalks. With blaring horns, screaming cabbies, and thousands of voices all talking at the same time, could Buddy keep her mind on her

Morris Frank and Buddy. Their journey would open the doors of the world for millions. (Photo courtesy of SeeingEye.org.)

job? Block by block, with the press verbally marveling
at her skills, the dog took her master from store to
store and corner to corner. They met challenges such
as riding an elevator, getting on a bus, and navigating Grand Central Terminal. That should have been
enough proof, but the requests kept coming. When it
was suggested the pair cross a busy eight-lane street,
Morris took the challenge. He was no more than ten
feet off the curb when he realized he'd made a mistake
and was in far over his head. There were huge trucks,
buses, and cars roaring all around him. As the man became more unnerved, the dog moved ahead, stopped
when it saw an oncoming vehicle, waited for the mo-
torized giant to pass, sometimes even pushing Morris
back a few steps, then when it was safe, resumed the
trek. It took several minutes and a dozen different
stops in the middle of the crowded thoroughfare, but
with loud applause coming from the hundreds who
had stopped to watch the display of a guide dog in
action, Morris and Buddy finally stepped up safely
on the opposite curb. The story of the short journey
would be printed in newspapers all around the globe.

For the next few days, Morris and Buddy were the
toast of Broadway. They were interviewed by several
newspapers and magazines and were invited to hotels,
restaurants, and plays. Their photos were taken, and

people even asked for Morris's autograph. But there were still challenges to be met.

Before leaving New York, a blind man ridiculed the guide and owner as nothing more than a dog-and-pony show. He sarcastically announced, "It's bad enough being blind without being tied to a dog." He and hundreds of others saw the whole affair as a gimmick and refused to listen when Morris preached, "You are not tied to the dog; you are freed by it."

While Buddy was a celebrity in New York, she was usually looked at as just another mutt when the pair left the Big Apple. The railroad lines even made the canine ride in a baggage car. On those parts of the trip, Morris was again blind and had to depend upon others to help him find his way around the train.

In Nashville, with Buddy leading the way, Morris moved with an ease and speed he had not known since before he lost his sight. Going to work, to school, and on social outings was a breeze. The local interest created by the unusual sight of a dog leading a man also helped Morris sell more insurance policies and meet more people. More important, the press ate up news of the dog and his value to Morris. The stories that ran in newspapers and magazines generated so much mail that the young man soon spent as much time answering correspondence as he did working.

Each letter was as different as the person who penned it. Preachers explained how they could no longer visit their flocks due to their blindness. Businessmen wrote of not being able to travel to meet clients or make sales outside the office. Lawyers informed Morris of their inability to travel to meetings and courts without human help. Housewives and students sent letters, as did farmers and teachers. They all spoke of the limitations their disabilities had created, the burden they had become to others, and the way their potential was being dismissed. Most of all they wanted to know how they could get a dog to help them regain their independence.

Being the first brings a bright spotlight. It also generates tremendous responsibilities. Morris quickly felt the weight of both. He had so greatly benefited from Buddy that he felt an obligation to share his blessings with others. Remembering the pledge he had received from Eustis and Humphrey, Morris contacted them. He explained how Buddy had proved her value and then shared the letters from those looking for a way to rediscover their independence. Sensing she had chosen the right person to sell this revolutionary program, Eustis provided some initial funding. She also sent Humphrey to Nashville to train the guide dogs. In the midst of the Great Depression, when millions around

the nation had lost all hope, a school called The Seeing
Eye was established to bring hope to those who could
not see. Within a year, the school was so successful
that it had outgrown its initial facility and moved to
New Jersey.

Morris and Buddy spent the next decade traveling
from coast to coast and border to border. They lobbied
state and federal governments and met with thousands of business leaders. At each stop they fought for
the rights of the disabled and lobbied to allow service dogs on trains, airplanes, and ships, as well as in
restaurants, hotels, offices, and all other public buildings. Largely because of Buddy's amazing abilities, the
pair changed attitudes, gave hope to the millions, and
opened the eyes of those with perfect vision to the
potential of those who were disabled.

By 1938, Buddy was the best-known dog in the
world. Her work had been the driving force behind
more changes in legislation and education than perhaps any lawmaker of her era. When she died, thousands of letters and telegrams poured in from all over
the world. But the nationwide recognition of the dog's
passing was less about what had been lost through
death than it was about what had been gained through
her life. This dog had opened up the world to millions.

Essentially, Buddy led society out of a dark time

when the disabled were written off and into an era when they were recognized not by their disabilities but for their talents and potential. Therefore, everyone who has benefited and gained independence through the use of a service dog, as well as the millions those people have touched, owes a great deal to a dog named Buddy. When this German shepherd put her best paw forward, she was ultimately leading the world in a brand-new direction.

Finding Love

Love isn't something you find. Love is something that finds you.
Loretta Young

They say love is blind. And those who find it never see what hit them. It seems to strike most often when you are not seeking it. But for most, they must be led to love to finally be led by it. And cupid does not always take the form of a cherub.

Tierra Amarilla, a small, unincorporated community near the Carson National Forest in northern New Mexico, is a place that bridges time. If you stand in just the right place, it seems you can see forever, and yet as you strain your eyes to take in the view, a person is almost always struck by the feeling of isolation. Set at an elevation of over seven thousand feet means the air in Tierra Amarilla is thin and the vegetation sparse. In the distance, inhospitable mountains beckon and the ghosts of generations who sought and failed to find riches on those rocky points seem to cry out every time the wind blows. This is the Old West seen in John Wayne movies and incorporated into Zane Grey novels. It has been captured in paintings and on postcards and served to inspire countless songs. A quick glance reveals the influence of ancient Americans, Mexican immigrants, and the American Depression. There were so many vacant and decaying buildings that this small city was often called a ghost town.

It took a special breed to meet the challenges created by the tiny community's isolation and environment, and Joseph Martinez was just such a man. He embraced an optimistic nature and managed to smile when faced with the summer's unrelenting heat as well as the winter's frigid cold and relished the challenges that caused others to pack up and leave. He was both realist and optimist, two qualities that sustained him in the inhospitable world he and his family called home. More than anything else, he was a builder who could fix anything. Yet he would soon be greeted by a problem that was beyond his abilities to address.

In the dark winter days of 1977, Joseph and his

wife, Terri, were overjoyed to find out they would
be having another child. When that bright June day
came to welcome the newest member in the Martinez
family, it was a time of great celebration in the small
community. The beautiful little girl, who the parents
named Jamie, was a bright, active, curious baby who
quickly learned to talk in both Spanish and English.
She was beyond a doubt the perfect child the family
had prayed for and dreamed of. Yet just as dreams
and nightmares often violently collided in the harsh
world around Tierra Amarilla, the family would soon
find darkness in the midst of light. An unseen and
unknown enemy had been there since the moment
Jamie's DNA was spun. It was now on the prowl, and,
because of its reach, the family's world was about to be
turned upside down.

Jamie was eighteen months old when the family
physician noted something was amiss. The tests that
followed revealed an issue with Jamie's vision. More
exams discovered the cause. The invisible monster
lurking inside the child had a name, making it sound
as if it had come from another planet—retinitis pigmentosa. Just the way those two words rolled off the
tongue was almost as numbing as the look on the
doctor's face when he said them.

Up until that point, the Martinez family had no

knowledge of the genetic disorder that affects the retina's ability to respond to light. Thus, even as the diagnosis settled in, the couple initially hoped the specialist would offer a way to combat what he called RP. Their hopes were quickly crushed. There was no cure, and in a matter of just a few years, the child who seemed so perfect and healthy would be completely blind. Dreams had been dashed, and suddenly, even though she was just a toddler, Jamie's life had limits.

It is said the greatest fear is created not by things you can see but by that which you don't see. For parents this fear is magnified tenfold when it is your child who will be battling in the dark. Sadly, there was no escape as the reminders of that image were everywhere. From his home, as he looked out at the mountains, Joseph realized that soon his child would not be able to view the awesome beauty. She would also not be able to see the yellow clay beneath her feet or the pure whiteness of a fresh winter snow. And then there were the dangers that, if not seen, could prove deadly.

As the Martinez family attempted to cope with the devastating news, as they tried to foresee things they would be facing in the future, there were whispers in the community. People were saying that Jamie's RP was a punishment from God for something the family had done. The gossip, while painful, was certainly not something the Martinez family took to heart, but it also didn't offer any comfort, hope, or support. So, in many ways, they were on an island dealing with something they had no experience in handling.

As the parents battled doubts and fears, Jamie eagerly went on about life. She had things to learn and a world to explore. For the time being, she also had her eyesight. And though it was gradually fading, she adapted, and in time so did Joseph and Terri. And perhaps due to the harsh conditions found in the region they called home, the parents understood that people had to be tough to survive, not just the challenges brought on by limited opportunities, extreme weather, and the rugged terrain but also those challenges created by physical disabilities. For Jamie to succeed, it was going to take grit; so when she fell, they encouraged her to get back up on her own. Time and time again, the little girl proved she was not a quitter. She always found ways to adapt and succeed. So buoyed by their daughter's "I can do anything" attitude, Joseph and Terri quickly began to treat her just like their other children. The older she got, the more they allowed her to embrace a sense of independence. Their attitudes were a godsend for the bright-eyed youngster; still, nothing could prevent each day of Jamie's life from getting a little darker. By fifth grade the awe-inspiring mountains were nothing but shadows, and her friends were no longer seen as much as heard.

As her world grew darker, her parents sensed it was time to find Jamie more help than was available in Tierra Amarilla. They realized if she stayed in the community, there would be no chance for independence or any opportunity to fully realize her potential. With that reality driving their thoughts, they made a huge leap of faith. Though the girl had become the light in Joseph's and Terri's lives, it was their love for their child who motivated them to send Jamie almost 400 miles south to the New Mexico State School for the Blind in Alamogordo.

Though initially homesick, Jamie thrived in the school. Placed in an independent study plan suited to her specific needs, she quickly became more confident. Like a sponge she soaked up her classwork while also learning Braille and how to navigate with a cane. In a world where she was just like everyone else, she ran track, played ball games adapted for the visually impaired, and learned to ski. The school was more than just a place to grow; for six years it was a safe, comfortable home. Though her test scores and grades seemed to prove she was ready for college, could Jamie leave the bubble and make her mark in a world not set up to address her specific disability, or would she opt for the safety net and go home to live with her parents? Just like her father relished the challenges of life in the rugged mountains and plains of northern New Mexico, Jamie gritted her teeth and met an unknown world head on.

Within weeks of beginning her studies at New Mexico State University (NMSU), the confident young woman fully understood the great limitations created by her blindness in a world built for sighted people. In the small town where she was raised, there were people who watched her grow up and looked out for the blind person. At the School for the Blind she was protected and accepted. But in her new environment, most people had never known a blind person. Many were so intimidated by her disability that it was not easy for the blind freshman to make friends. On top of that, her coursework often didn't offer alternatives for the visually impaired. While the toughness instilled in her by her parents wouldn't let her quit, she was struggling to find ways to adapt and be accepted. As she somehow willed her way through each new day, she had no way of knowing a hero would soon march into her world and bring her a formula that included so much more than just independence. In fact, this canine champion would reroute her entire life.

Long before Jamie was born, her special needs

were being addressed. In 1942, Lois Merrihew and Don Donaldson had the vision. The pair founded a school in Los Gantos, California, to train dogs to serve as guides for the visually impaired. Though Guide Dogs for the Blind was inspired by the injuries that soldiers, marines, and airmen sustained fighting the battles of World War II, the school quickly expanded to serve the needs of those blinded by accident and disease. More than fifty years after it was founded, at a time when Jamie Martinez was fighting to gain her independence, the school was training a yellow Labrador retriever named Fresca. That dog would soon dramatically change the college student's life.

Fresca had been bred in the school's kennels with one purpose in mind: to be a blind person's eyes. Raised by volunteers for a year, she was then returned to the school to undergo several months of rigorous and challenging training necessary to earn the title "Guide Dog." When the harness was in place, she was all business and ready to work. When the harness was taken off, she was a well-behaved dog, eager to play.

It was 1996 when a nervous Jamie got on a plane and flew to the Pacific Northwest. She hoped that a guide dog would be the answer to living a life not limited by her lack of vision. Unsure but optimistic, alone in a strange place surrounded by people she didn't

know, the college student met the dog specifically chosen to fit her needs.

The first time she felt the Lab's wet nose against her
arm and held Fresca's broad head in her hands, it was
love at first touch. She'd come to San Rafael, California, on a wing and prayer, and she sensed her chances
to succeed would be greatly increased by this happy
canine.

Sitting beside Jamie on that first night were several other sight-impaired people looking for help.
One was a young man from Texas. Wayne Sibson had
become blind at the age of ten, and, as this was his
second guide dog, he already had learned how much
a dog could expand his horizons. As Jamie and Wayne
became acquainted with their dogs and learned the
fundamentals of working as a team, Fresca and Hathaway, Wayne's new dog, bonded as well.

Though Jamie didn't fully grasp it, it wasn't just
Wayne's dog who wanted to spend time with Fresca;
the University of Texas graduate was also looking for
excuses to hang out with the coed from New Mexico State. Wayne found ways for the two to eat meals
together and spend both training time and downtime
in the same places.

A month of rigorous training put Fresca and Jamie
into every conceivable life situation from shopping

to being dropped off in an unknown area and being expected to find their way back to the assigned rendezvous point. The dog performed perfectly in every test, but like most first-time students, it took Jamie a while to fully trust her new eyes. By the time graduation rolled around, and the new team headed southwest, the woman and dog worked together almost seamlessly.

Back at NMSU, the dog was excited but confident, while the human wondered if the grand experiment would really work. Folding up her cane, it was time to test the waters.

Starting with her first day on campus, Fresca immediately changed Jamie's life. With her cane, long treks across campus were an ordeal. The white stick simply couldn't warn her about every obstacle in her path or alert her to a host of other things a sighted person noted each day. On top of that, a woman swinging a cane could be intimidating for those in her path.

From the moment they stepped out the door, Fresca allowed Jamie to move with confidence. Her stride was longer and more secure. She had no fear of running into something or hitting someone. As the dog got to know the campus, the trips from place to place became easier. In fact, Fresca always wanted to explore and see new things, which led Jamie to places and events she'd avoided in the past. This expansion of her world is why she'd wanted the dog, but there was another benefit that she hadn't imagined.

Fresca was a people magnet. Because of Jamie's blindness and cane, in the past, other students had shied away from her. Perhaps it was because they didn't know what to say, or perhaps they were intimidated, but now everyone wanted to know Fresca. Suddenly it seemed Jamie was the most popular person on campus. She couldn't go anywhere without people introducing themselves and asking questions. With her guide dog serving as the icebreaker, these new acquaintances discovered they had a great deal in common with the blind coed. So with the dog now offering more than security and navigation, Fresca enlarged Jamie's circle of friends and therefore her influence. In a very real sense, thanks to her dog, the young woman was an emerging star at NMSU as well as a willing ambassador of the unlimited potential for those who were blind.

While Jamie was using Fresca to move forward, in Austin, Texas, another Guide Dog graduate was reflecting on his days in San Rafael. In fact, Wayne Sibson couldn't get Jamie out of his mind. When he wasn't at work, he was thinking about her all the time. He even found himself sharing his thoughts with his dog. It was Hathaway who provided an excuse for a second meeting with Jamie. In the fall of 1997, Wayne made a trip to NMSU so the guide dogs who had enjoyed each other's company so much in California could get reacquainted. It didn't take long for Jamie to figure out Wayne was interested in more than just a puppy reunion. While that was flattering, the young woman had other things on her mind. On the merits of her coursework, she had earned an internship working with Senator Jeff Bingaman in Washington, DC. With an adventure at the capital calling, love was not an option she wanted to consider. So, for a second time it seemed, Wayne had struck out.

Washington, DC, was not just a long distance from Tierra Amarilla, New Mexico; from landscape to environment, the two couldn't have been more different. While her hometown was wide open and laid back, her new world was teeming with people and activity, offering a myriad of challenges that would frighten most sighted college students. In an atmosphere filled with noise, traffic, and people speaking a dozen different languages, Fresca navigated as easily as she had at NMSU. Nothing distracted her when she was on harness. Yet once more, the yellow Lab's skill set went well beyond getting from point A to point B. With her smiling muzzle and bright eyes, the ambassador with a wagging tail continued her role as an icebreaker. From the Capitol Building to the supermarket, everyone wanted to know more about the canine serving as Jamie's eyes. They were constantly the center of attention and made friends with everyone from the janitorial staff to the highest-ranking members of Congress.

One of the funniest moments came when Senator Ted Kennedy introduced himself and asked if he could pet Fresca. Jamie was conflicted, since no one was supposed to pet a guide dog in harness, yet this was a legendary senator and she was just a college intern, so she said yes. Another time, her own boss, Jeff Bingaman Jr. approached Fresca and attempted to give her a treat. Finding her voice and using the diplomacy she learned during her brief tenure in Washington, Jamie announced, "Sorry, no, you can't." Then she explained why.

The summer in DC assured Jamie she could go anywhere and do anything. In fact, thanks to her guide dog, the young woman sensed she had an advantage in initiating friendships and creating meaningful and deep relationships. People seemed to be drawn to her. She began to realize that her loss of sight might be providing her a deeper insight into reading people's minds, voices, and hearts. She could hear emotions where others couldn't even see them. It was obvious from her empathic nature that Fresca could, too. Thus, Jamie's major in counseling seemed a perfect fit for the strengths of the woman and her guide.

After returning to New Mexico, Jamie had a new resolve to finish her degree and to locate a graduate school to deepen her knowledge. With trying to stay fixated on that goal, one person, accompanied by his guide dog, kept returning and interrupting her life. Though she continued to emphasize that she was focused solely on her career, her unasked-for suitor was not going to give up. After all, he argued, their dogs loved each other and the animals should get to see each other from time to time. As happy as Fresca and Hathaway were to see each other on an even more regular basis, Jamie soon had to admit she was just as thrilled to be with Wayne. Still, it was difficult to think beyond just friendship.

A part of her fear of giving in to love was lodged in the fact that two blind people would face obstacles that offered far more challenges and risks than climbing the mountains around her hometown. Could a relationship thrive under those conditions? Besides, there was also the question of value. No matter how many times she'd proved herself in school, without vision, could she fully measure up as a wife and mother?

It was Fresca who supplied that answer and quelled her doubts. The dog had proved there was nothing Jamie couldn't do or places she couldn't go as long she had someone she trusted walking beside her. Time and time again the guide dog had proved she didn't have to settle for anything. So thanks to the yellow Lab leading, the young woman allowed her emotions to trump the world's perceptions. She would and could find a way to adapt; the sense she had lost was more than made up for by what she had gained. Thus, brimming with confidence, she made the choice to say yes to love.

With Hathaway serving as the ring bearer, the two were married. Shocking everyone but their dogs, on their honeymoon in the Bahamas, the couple swam, parasailed, and explored. It was another new adventure, one that few would expect a blind couple to make; but thanks to their guide dogs and their own heightened senses, they "saw" the beauty and wonder of this new world while wrapped in the love that their canine matchmakers, Fresca and Hathaway, saw long before either of them did. It was the couple's blindness, along with an assist supplied by a pair of four-pawed cupids, that made it all happen.

Today Jamie and Wayne work in Austin, own a home, and have two children, Jordyn and Kamryn.

Jamie is now being led by her third guide dog. Those dogs have been more than her eyes; they have also helped raise her children. Yet it was Jamie's first dog, Fresca, who really changed everything. It was that yellow Lab who introduced her to her future husband, brought her to see a world with unlimited opportunity, expanded her friendships, and took her from her small New Mexico hometown to the center of the world's most powerful government. In the process, the dreams that Joseph had for his daughter—dreams that once seemed crushed by a diagnosis of retinitis pigmentosa—were not just realized, they were exceeded.

Team Potential

Individual commitment to a group effort—that is what makes a team work, a company work, a society work, a civilization work.

Vince Lombardi

A world without sound is a very lonely place. Not being able to hear a phone or a doorbell brings on a sense of isolation that few can imagine. The silence is overwhelming, and the fear that accompanies it can be numbing. Worst of all, so many tend to judge harshly because they don't understand that you simply can't hear them when they call. That quiet isolation creates depression and crushes hope.

Ames, Iowa, is a long way from Puerto Rico, but in the fall of 2002, this rural, midwestern college town was the most important place on earth for one eighteen-year-old woman. Cristina Saint-Blancard, a newly minted Iowa State University (ISU) freshman, was experiencing the rewards of devoting her time and effort to building an outstanding academic résumé. The bright-eyed, attractive recent high school grad, whose smile lit up every room she entered and whose Puerto Rican accent was greeted with fascination in the middle of the Corn Belt, was ready and prepared to pursue a dream. She had not chosen an easy path to success, as she was seeking a degree in the male-dominated discipline of mechanical engineering.

Cristina's father, Alexander, an engineer, and mother, Teresa, a teacher, had long prayed their daughter would find an educational outlet that would challenge her to fully use her drive and talents, and ISU seemed the perfect answer to those prayers. Still, even after having their daughter settle into her new home at Friley Hall and easily make friends with everyone she met, the couple could not cast aside all their worries. Since early childhood, Cristina had been plagued by asthma and recurrent infections. At times the attacks were so severe that the child would get treated in the emergency room. In the past she had been fine because they were always there. But would she be able to handle an attack without them to help her? Would her new friends know what to do?

Cristina's first semester flew by. From pep rallies to football games to lab work, Cristina cherished each new experience. And even though her heavy coursework was challenging, it still seemed as if she had been magically transported to a place filled with wonder and excitement. This seemed to be fully proved when she looked out her dormitory window and spied snow for the first time in her life. With others looking at her as if she were crazy, the Puerto Rico native raced outside trying to catch the fluffy white flakes on her tongue. Giggling like a child, she made snow angels, built snowmen, and participated in a snowball fight. There was simply no way for her to explain that first winter adventure to her friends back home. She also found no words to tell her high school friends what it was like to experience four very different seasons.

The joy of her four years in college and the bonds she made with her professors and fellow students ended much too quickly. Yet long nights in the library and more hours spent studying in her room had paid off. When she graduated in 2006, she was invited to Ohio State University for graduate school. Although she hated to leave behind the place that had been the bridge from youth to adulthood and had pushed her to seek her full potential, she couldn't wait to attack the next step in what was proving to be an outstanding academic career.

In many ways Columbus, Ohio, was not that much different from Ames. Both were communities built around a passion for their universities. School colors lined the streets, and everyone talked about the local teams. Thus, the transition was as smooth as her move to college. It is hardly surprising that the outgoing Cristina immediately found friends and carved out a place where she was comfortable. As she pursued her postgraduate degree in biomedical engineering, she did research in a hospital's neonatal intensive care unit and became aware of the need for volunteers to rock infants born to drug addicts. Cristina was deeply drawn to the plight of children who were craving the same drugs their mothers used during pregnancy. Just the act of holding them brought out sincere empathy and deep compassion that were as elusive to explain as the way a snowflake had felt on her tongue four years before. There was a draw in this work that touched her soul in ways she didn't fully understand. And while her soft words and gentle touch brought a bit of peace to each child, holding them also gave her a sense of deep sadness. Through no fault of their own, they were struggling to survive. She couldn't have guessed that she would soon find herself in the very same position.

As weeks became months and scores of babies found comfort in the grad student's arms, Cristina suddenly became sick. This was not just another asthma attack like she experienced in her youth; this was something much worse. Tests revealed a bacterial infection was waging war on her body. She had likely picked it up while volunteering to rock infants at the hospital. Admitted as a patient, she developed such a high fever that Cristina found herself fighting for her life. Thanks to her medical team and her own strength, she would win that battle, but the victory would come with a high cost. The vibrant young woman was now deaf. Too weak to continue her education and unprepared to cope with a life in a now-silent world, Cristina was forced to withdraw from school and move to Florida where her parents lived and could help her with her many hospitalizations.

Initially Cristina figured that once she regained her strength and understood how to deal with deafness, her life would return to normal. Yet it was soon apparent the infection had created other serious and life-threatening problems. With no warning signs her vertigo was exacerbated. She could be walking through a room or carrying on a conversation when extreme dizziness would set in. For a few seconds the world would violently spin, and then she'd pass out.

In a period of months, because of the falls created by vertigo, she suffered several broken bones, concussions, and deep head wounds. She found herself in the emergency room so often that doctors and nurses knew her by sight. But the deafness and vertigo were just the beginning of her problems.

The asthma and recurrent infections that had plagued her in childhood returned with a vengeance. With no warning it would be all but impossible for the young woman to breathe. The attacks grew more and more frequent and violent, some happening while she was out in public. When combined with the vertigo and hearing loss, the asthma made her all but homebound. She was in bed more than she was up, and because of her inactivity, she began to put on more weight. That weight gain further aggravated her other health issues. Within months she had become morbidly obese, which made her asthma attacks even worse and the vertigo more dangerous.

The woman whose life once had such great promise could no longer get out of her home without help, and just walking from room to room was a monumental accomplishment. Unable to hear the phone ring or understand her parents' voices, alone in a world without sound, she was depressed and lonely. Rather than level off or get better, her condition continued to worsen. As she grew heavier, doctors suggested the family prepare for a funeral.

Though there were times she could hardly breathe, though she was cut off from the music of the world and all but homebound, Cristina was not a quitter. She'd worked hard to get through college, and throughout her life, her dynamic determination had allowed her to knock down every roadblock. Her doctors were amazed by the way she fought back from infections that would have been fatal for most people. But the sad fact was that they had done all they could do. For Cristina to live just a few more years, she was going to need a miracle, and that miracle would not come through medical science.

When all hope is gone, where do you look for answers? As she struggled to breathe and walk, Cristina thought back to the babies she had rocked. They were plunged into a world in which their own mothers craved a drug more than the love of their children. It was no wonder these babies cried so much. They were fighting for life and calling out for love and acceptance. And yet they grew quiet and calm in Cristina's arms. In a way, she gave them security, hope, and a sense of value. If only someone could do that for her.

The past few months of illness had reshaped Cristina's vision of the world. When she tried to communicate with people in stores, because of her hearing loss, most had no patience in dealing with her. They often treated the incredibly gifted woman as if she were stupid. The vertigo and breathing issues also drove people away from her. The fact that her illnesses had caused a great weight gain brought both judgment and ridicule. She longed for hope and acceptance, but no one seemed to offer either. Each day she found herself more isolated, and it seemed there was nothing that could be humanly done to change that depressing fact.

Cristina and her parents were at the end of their ropes when a Canine Companions' volunteer puppy raiser from Ohio suggested she look into getting a hearing dog. While that dog couldn't fix her vertigo or cure her asthma, because of its special training, it could become her ears. Realizing her deafness was keeping her from fully noticing the world around her, Cristina contacted Canine Companions for Independence. The organization interviewed Cristina, studied her medical issues, and agreed to work with her. In June of 2011, hope and acceptance came in the form a black Labrador/golden retriever mix named Tatiana.

As she walked up to meet Cristina, the dog's eyes were filled with love. She didn't care about Cristina's weight or her inability to hear. She was there to offer love and service, and from the minute she came through the door, her focus was on the woman she'd been sent to help. Within an hour the bond had been formed, and it was all but impossible to pry Tatiana from the sick woman's side. Yet it would be over the next few days that the power of the dog's long and extensive training was completely revealed.

Since she had lost almost all her hearing, Cristina had been on an island. She couldn't hear and therefore didn't notice much of what was going on inside her home or outside the front door. Now, thanks to Tatiana, when the phone rang, Cristina immediately found out. She also was alerted when someone was at the door, the microwave was finished cooking, or the alarm clock buzzed. When they ventured outside, Tatiana did something even more special; she opened up a line of communication. Because of the dog's wagging tail and lopsided grin, people were attracted to her. Thus, rather than grow impatient when trying to communicate with the deaf woman, they listened more intently and were glad to slowly repeat anything Cristina didn't understand. This unexpected bonus brought bright rays of sunshine into what had become a very dark and lonely world. For the first time in what seemed like forever, the woman was being accepted by society. Working in tandem with a canine does not happen overnight.

While the dog can perform all the tasks taught at school and thus greatly enhance the life of its partner, it is only when the canine grows to really know the human's personality that the real magic begins.

The first time Tatiana showed any signs of real distress was when Cristina experienced a bout of vertigo and tumbled to the ground. As Tatiana had been trained to be Cristina's ears, the dog was simply not prepared for this. Frantic and worried, Tatiana stayed with the woman until she was able to stand. Still anxious and likely confused, the dog then walked the woman back to safety. The next time the vertigo struck, the results were the same. Tatiana was concerned, obviously troubled, and confused. Yet even though the episodes upset her, the dog never shied away.

A few days later, Cristina was walking outside the house when, for no apparent reason, Tatiana pushed her toward a bench. As the woman was breathing easily and completely focused on the world around her, she didn't want to sit down. The dog wouldn't give up, continuing to use her shoulder to gently direct Cristina to a spot she felt she needed to be. A few seconds after she sat down, the vertigo, which was initially caused by Ménière's disease, hit. Only after it passed did Cristina begin to wonder if Tatiana had somehow sensed the attack was coming. A few days later, when the dog again forced the woman to take a seat just before an attack hit, it was obvious the dog read something in Cristina's body language that even she couldn't read.

The knowledge that Tatiana could alert Cristina to a fire alarm, a siren, or a coming storm, as well as warn her before vertigo stuck, brought a great deal of security to the home. No longer did Alexander and Teresa have to worry about leaving their daughter alone. And thanks to Cristina no longer taking tumbles during attacks, the young woman was escaping life-threatening injuries. How the dog became a vertigo forecaster is something that no one, including the trainers at Canine Companions, could explain. Yet this adaptive skill would pale when compared to the dog's next intuitive action.

Just a month after Tatiana came into Cristina's life, the woman began having such severe breathing issues, brought on by another infection, that her parents took her to the emergency room. The medical staff treated Cristina and kept her under observation until her body signs returned to normal. Once they were convinced the crisis had passed, she was sent home. Except for a bit of weakness, the woman felt fine when she went to bed. As had become her habit, Tatiana took her place beside the woman she served.

It was around 3:00 a.m. when the dog put her front paws on the bed and nosed Cristina. Tatiana's actions were not unusual; she often rose on her hind legs to check on the woman. Though no one will ever know if it was through observation or some type of instinctive sense, the dog rushed from the room and raced through the home to the bedroom where Cristina's parents were sleeping. The suddenly shocked couple was awakened by frantic nudging, which Tatiana was trained to do to alert Cristina to sounds, and the body language of a canine who obviously wanted them to follow her. As the couple rose from their bed, the black dog rushed back to Cristina's room with the parents jogging behind. As Alexander flipped on the lights, his heart sank. His daughter was deathly still, her face pale and her lips almost blue. Checking her pulse, he discovered that her heart had stopped and she wasn't breathing. As Teresa called the EMTs, he began to administer CPR, but Cristina was still showing no signs of life when the ambulance arrived.

With a frantic dog and two worried parents looking on, the paramedics quickly went to work; and within a minute, their patient was breathing. Once she was stabilized, the ambulance rushed Cristina to the hospital. After examining the woman, the emergency room physician assured Alexander and Teresa their daughter should make a full recovery, but if she'd gone without help for a minute more, she would surely have suffered brain damage. It was at that moment the dog's role as a lifesaver was fully realized.

The severe, silent, and almost fatal asthma attack kept Cristina in the hospital for a week. When she finally returned home, all she wanted to do was remain in her bed, but the dog had other ideas. In Tatiana's mind it was time to get moving.

It was time to meet more challenges. The bacterial infection had forced the woman to give up on a dream. And although she still had numerous health issues, soon after receiving Tatiana, Cristina decided to return to school and study for her master's degree at Purdue University. Her health was still fragile, her recurrent infections and asthma attacks still created severe issues, and she was legally deaf. Could someone with all those obstacles live independently and find a way to succeed at school? The logical answer was a resounding no. But in truth she wasn't doing this alone, and Tatiana would be with her every step of the way. With the dog by her side, the woman was convinced she could beat the odds. When Cristina was asked how she could balance all her health issues with a full school schedule, she explained she was just trying to keep up with her role model, Tatiana. Time and time again the woman told her friends, "The dog epitomizes pure, selfless, and unconditional love. She lives in the moment, accepts people for who they are, and simply loves life. She is loyal and dependable and never holds grudges. If I could be half the person my dog is, I'd be twice the human I am." In other words, Tatiana saw the woman's potential and kept pushing her to reach it.

In 2012, the American Humane Association named Tatiana the "Hearing Hero Dog of the Year." The black canine was singled out for saving her master's life. But the dog had done far more than that. She had reawakened Cristina's dreams, gotten her back into the world, and rebirthed her confidence, which led to the woman receiving her master's degree in biomedical engineering. Tatiana had become so well known and loved at Purdue, she led the woman across the stage when Purdue awarded the dog an honorary master's degree in friendship and guidance.

During this time, Cristina's sister had become a runner and was constantly training for everything from 5Ks to half marathons. When her sister invited them to cheer her on, it inspired Cristina to begin exercising, and she was hooked. With her dog leading the way and pacing her, over the next few months the walking turned into slow jogging. The more she exercised, the better she felt; and this motivated Cristina to push even harder. Ten pounds lost became twenty, twenty became fifty, and in a matter of two years, Cristina had lost more than 170 pounds and was running 5Ks with her sister.

Though she still is learning to live with deafness, though she is still plagued by attacks of both recurrent infections and heart issues, Cristina is running half marathons and has become an advocate for disability awareness and the use of service animals. She also works with people going through some of the same medical issues that have caused so much strife in her own life. She tells those struggling to get through the dark days, "While I know that I am in no way a failure, I cannot help but feel unaccomplished since my health issues constantly slow me down and have kept me from fulfilling my original goals and plans. So I may not be the person I thought I should be with the career I thought I should have, but I know in my heart that I am the person I was meant to be and can only hope that will inspire others to be the same."

And why has Cristina been able to reach so many with this message of hope? It is because of a dog who saved her life twice: the first time when she stopped breathing and the second time when Tatiana pushed her out of bed and back into living a full life. It took a team to make it happen, and the story is really just beginning.

Memories

Memories are the best things in life, I think.

Romy Schneider

The roads less traveled often lead us to unforgettable memories. Shared experiences along those roads create the most compelling memories. It is by holding onto those memories that we come to appreciate life fully.

More than six decades ago, Allen and Sharon Friedman met while students at the University of Minnesota. In the midst of football games, dances, and winter walks on campus, love bloomed. After two years of dating and Allen's graduation, they married and began a life filled with love and adventure. Allen served two years as an officer in the Medical Service

Corps and then did his graduate study in public administration. He then became a city manager before becoming a court administrator and finally the manager of a law firm.

Sharon, who devoted her life to social work, raised three daughters in a world without boundaries. They swam with manatees in Florida, went scuba diving with green moray eels in the Atlantic Ocean, photographed bears in Wyoming's Grand Tetons, sailed yachts in the Great Lakes and the Atlantic, and rode motorcycles across the Midwest. They viewed the places where history was made and gained perspective and appreciation for a wide variety of music, culture, and art. When Allen obtained his pilot's license and the couple purchased a plane, the family found an even greater freedom that expanded their already wide horizon. Trips that used to take days via car now took hours. Simply put, theirs was a life of their own design balanced between enjoying the wonders of the world in their free time and serving the needs of people through their work.

Not too many years after Allen and Sharon were married, Bill Withers wrote a song that was taken to the top of the rock-and-roll charts by Ben E. King. "Lean on Me" embraced a theme that was simple, direct, and positive. People simply couldn't make it by themselves. They had to have folks they could trust to help them through the tough times. In his song, Withers captured the essence of the magic that bound Allen and Sharon together. Their natural ability to lean on each other had seen them through the good times and would soon define a new phase of their lives.

It has long been noted that time flies when you're having fun, and such was the case with the Friedmans' lives. The years rushed by as they were constantly on the go, eternally active, and always thirsty to experience new things. Thus, their fiftieth anniversary caught them by surprise. Even with such a long list of adventures behind them, there were still so many more exploits to plan. Best of all, without the demands of a job, they had even more free time on their hands to enrich their lives and experience. Though they were in their seventies, it was time to make more memories.

At the core of the couple's existence was optimism. They believed their love brought with it a passion for life and a formula for youth. They sensed their life was a product of that love, and their touching others with hope and compassion symbolized an extension of that love. The couple was a team. When they were together, the bond was obvious. They almost moved and reacted as one. They also encouraged, supported, and pushed each other. They had no idea that the team approach that had so naturally and wonderfully shaped their lives would become so important in allowing Sharon to hang onto the memories they had created.

As the couple made new plans, Allen began to notice little things that didn't seem quite right. Sharon was suffering occasional memory lapses, which stood in direct contrast with her sharp mind that always kept him on track. As her mental lapses became more frequent, he began to worry. After a trip to the doctor, the test results delivered an almost unbelievable verdict. Sharon had the beginnings of Alzheimer's. Just hearing that word can be numbing, but then applying it to the one you love is crushing. Suddenly, making new memories didn't seem as important as hanging onto the ones they already had.

The Friedmans' collie, Schenley.

Alzheimer's, the cause of over half the dementia found in older people, is a chronic neurodegenerative disease that begins slowly, almost like a child learning to crawl, and over time, picks up speed. Sharon's disease was spotted because she was having difficulty remembering recent events, but the couple was told that, as time passed, the disease would also lead to mood swings and complete withdrawal. Worst of all, there was no known cause and absolutely no cure.

In spite of the overwhelming nature of facing Sharon's life expectancy of only three to nine years, the Friedmans had an advantage that most could not claim. Thanks in large part to Allen's noting the initial and very subtle changes in his wife's responses, Sharon's Alzheimer's had been diagnosed early. Likely even more important was that the Mayo Clinic was in their backyard. Thus, they had access to the best doctors, latest research, and breakthrough medications.

Reaction, response, and attitude are huge keys in facing any life issue. Sharon knew that from her years in social work. Thus, rather than hunker down and wait for the worst, the Friedmans optimistically relished each new day they were given and continued the life and adventures they had already planned. Amazingly, as the months turned into years, somehow the disease was kept at bay, and Sharon continued to enjoy life much as she had before the diagnosis. Ultimately, it wasn't the Alzheimer's but something far different that threatened to push her away from the active life she still relished.

Back pain restricted her mobility. Surgery, which was supposed to help, only made matters worse. Just moving a certain way brought on shooting pain that caused her to lose her balance. Because her back created problems with movement, Sharon also couldn't see or gauge when pavement was uneven or there was a drop-off in her path. Her stumbling created sudden jolts that brought on numbing pain. Allen didn't feel it was safe for his wife to walk around the house or yard without him being there to catch her if she stumbled or help her up if she fell. So essentially he became Sharon's crutch, and she constantly had to lean on him. Unable to be there for her every moment of every day and wanting to keep the door of independence somewhat open for Sharon, Allen began to look for alternatives.

It was almost by chance that Allen found out about mobility dogs. As he dug into the dogs' varied roles, he began to wonder if the answer to getting his wife out into public was not a human but a specially trained canine. When he considered the scope of Sharon's health issues, the thought seemed outlandish, but when you are grasping at straws to save a loved one, you will try almost anything.

A mobility dog fills a similar role as that of a guide dog. The dogs used in this role are usually large and athletic, and thanks to their size and strength, they have been largely successful when teamed with those suffering from crippling diseases such as Parkinson's disease and multiple sclerosis. Many pull wheelchairs or pick up objects for people who can't get up on their own. Others provide balance and stability for a person who can walk but has impairments that affect balance or strength. The dog can follow a command and even help a person out of a chair. While the dog does not serve as a crutch, the animal does provide help with balance and gait. The animal's skill set includes opening doors and cabinets and even turning on light switches. The dog is also trained to note things in a path, such as small impressions in the grass and cracks in the pavement, that might cause a person to trip or fall. Thus the dog becomes more than a guide; it is also there to anticipate and avoid issues that might lead to injuries. Like all service dogs, mobility dogs respond to verbal commands, and that was the one area Allen feared would keep the Friedmans from being able to use a dog to assist Sharon.

With the progression of Alzheimer's, there would

be times when his wife would not be able to remember the proper command for the action she needed at that moment. Without the right verbal cues, the dog would not be able to respond in the manner needed, and that lack of response might lead to frustration for both Sharon and the animal. Even with this stumbling block in his path, the man would not give up on the idea until he had spoken to the various training facilities that matched dogs with people. It was finally a call that came from a couple of thousand miles away that brought him some hope.

Kings Valley Collies, where Leslie Rappaport's school was located, trained dogs in much the same way as other institutions. It was a positive reward system that relied on praise rather than punishment. Like other schools, the commands the dogs learned hinged on vocal cues. Through the use of a specific word, the disabled person would tell the dog what he or she wanted and the dog would carry out that command. By the time a dog was placed with a person, the canine had a working vocabulary of more than fifty words. The animal's vocabulary grew to include more commands once it was accustomed to its new environment and the specific needs of the person it served. So while instinct and observation played a part in how the dog reacted, the partnership was based on verbal commands.

As Leslie finished explaining how things worked, Allen gave the trainer a rundown of the issues Sharon was dealing with, including Alzheimer's. He explained that because of the progression of the disease slowly eating up his wife's memory, vocal commands simply wouldn't work. Therefore, the option of using a dog to help her get out of a chair, to take a walk, or to safely attend outings with friends seemed out of the question.

Leslie was not about to shut the door just because of the unique parameters created by Alzheimer's. Instead, she looked at Sharon's case as a challenge that a good trainer should be able to address and assured Allen they could find a way to make this marriage of dog and woman work.

More than twenty-five years of training mobility dogs and placing them with clients had taught Leslie a great deal. Every situation was unique, and therefore every dog had to be educated to deal with the limitations and needs of the person he or she was to be matched with. In Sharon's case the dog was going to have to read the woman's body language and anticipate her needs. Everyone who had ever watched the *Lassie* TV series had seen Lassie respond in that way hundreds of times, but that dog was actually reacting to cues and commands coming from out of the camera's view. The canine partner Sharon Fried-man needed would be working without a script and a trainer. This dog would actually have to do what TV viewers believed Lassie did.

Leslie began by designing an entirely new train-ing method. When a person was in a chair or on the ground and needed to get up, the dog was going to have to read that need and put itself in the right po-sition to help. Body language, rather than a verbal command, was going to reveal when a person was losing his or her balance and needed support. The dog was also going to have to sense when a person was moving forward and wanted to stop. In other words, Sharon's dog was going have to be constantly studying her while continually reevaluating the environment. This dog was going to think!

Once Leslie understood the parameters, it was time to find the right dog. Though she had worked with several breeds, in this case, she was sure she needed a collie.

Collies have been bred for hundreds of years as herding dogs. They bond with the flock and are con-stantly studying the environment for potential dan-gers. They often work without commands. For centu-ries they have been expected to bring the flock or herd home before storms hit, to spot and fend off predators, to sense the weakest members of the group, and to pay close attention to the flock's needs. Collies also instinctively lean into those they are guiding in order to push them in the right direction. So it was the breed's ability to multitask, attentive nature and dynamic loyalty, and ability think and make quick decisions that assured Leslie this was the right choice for Sharon. But there was one drawback that automatically knocked out a majority of collies. While beautiful and distinctive, the breed's long, thick coats require a lot of attention. Most of those with whom she had placed collies had the time to meet this need, but this was a special case. A person with Alzheimer's and the caregiver would not likely have the time or energy for daily grooming. Leslie therefore decided that in this case she would use a smooth-coat collie.

Smooths are different from roughs, or Lassie-style collie, in one way: their coat is short like a standard German shepherd. Grooming them is easy. Other than that, they learn, respond, and react just like all the other members of their breed. Leslie had recently come upon a smooth that seemed the perfect choice to blaze a new trail for training methods and mobility expectations.

Schenley was a tricolor smooth who had been born in Canada. He was now a strong and outgoing young adult dog. While not show quality, he was intelligent, very people oriented, and eager to learn. Therefore, this collie seemed to possess all the characteristics needed for what some trainers would have viewed as the canine equivalent of *Mission Impossible*.

On trails, platforms, sidewalks, and every type of floor surface imaginable, Schenley was put through weeks of education. Working on a harness, Leslie silently imitated a person who was becoming dizzy or losing her balance. When Schenley responded in the correct manner, she praised him. Soon the perceptive dog could read a wide variety of body cues and respond to them. She then added vocal cues as a backup. By the time his training was completed, he had gained the ability to prevent falls, anticipate missteps, know when doors needed to be opened or closed, pick up dropped objects, and assist a person in rising from the floor or a chair. Most important, he was able to complete all of these and dozens of other tasks Sharon would require without any verbal cues.

When the black, white, and sable collie met Sharon, it was love at first sight. The woman was drawn to the dog, and when she seized the harness, Schenley immediately went to work. As an amazed Allen looked on, the dog helped Sharon up from her chair, guided her to the door, and slowly eased her down the steps and across the yard. Schenley sensed when she was faltering and, without prompting, leaned in, giving the support of his body. He then waited until he felt her touch on the harness to move forward. Over his first few weeks in the Friedmans' home, he reopened the world to Sharon.

Within weeks of Schenley's arrival, with the dog by her side, Sharon was back to visiting friends, attending plays and concerts, and living as independent a life as she had before her back issues. Sharon's condition even improved to the point where Allen could run errands and have no fear of leaving his wife at home. The collie took care of her needs, helped her get up and walk safely, prevented her from falling, and made sure she didn't wander away. Schenley also learned another vital skill. Even before Allen, he sensed when Sharon was not feeling well or her cognitive skills were out of sync. The dog was then able to alert the man when his wife needed extra care or should not be left alone.

Because Schenley has kept the door open, Sharon has been able to continue to visit her friends, and her mind has been able to hang on to the skill set she needs to communicate as well as reason. Thanks in large part to the happy dog's patient bearing and uplifting spirit, the woman has also held on to the optimistic spirit that has governed her entire life. This means that after sixty-two years of marriage, Allen and Sharon's union is still strong and meaningful, with both the husband and the wife knowing, loving, and appreciating each other. For many, that might not sound like much, but for those familiar with Alzheimer's, it is a miracle. Few with this disease live this long, and it is all but unheard of for one battling this disease to still be mentally participating in life.

When on harness, Schenley is like every other service dog; he is ready for duty and all business. In that capacity he has changed the Friedmans' lives and helped them create and hang on to new, wonderful memories. When the harness comes off, he is the family pet, but that does not end his looking for ways to serve. In his spare time, the collie has become the guide dog for their daughter's blind Labrador. He takes the Lab for walks in the nearby woods and makes sure he always safely returns home.

The question now becomes, is there potential for service dogs to do what medicines and other therapies cannot do in helping fight dementia? It is too early to tell, but Leslie Rappaport is already working on methods to train dogs to address the specific issues created by the disease. She has also shifted her training methods to teach all her mobility dogs to note and respond to body language and cues. Allen Friedman's unique challenge and Leslie's answer to that challenge have therefore opened the door to scores of people without verbal skills having mobility dogs that can assist them in their lives. So a collie who didn't measure up to show quality and a woman in need of a second chance set in motion a revolution that has the potential to impact thousands. That is something worth noting and remembering.

Employing Experience

Life can only be understood backwards; but it must be lived forwards.

Søren Kierkegaard

The experiences of youth have a profound impact on our future. What we see and learn as children often resurfaces to direct our actions and perspective as adults. When optimism reigns supreme in childhood, it tends to allow the mind to stay forever young.

Imagine growing up in a place where everyone was limited. Consider what it would be like only to exist in a small area where walls kept you in and others out. Ponder for a moment the thought of being a person everyone else saw as being so limited you are denied access to much of the real world. It was not that long ago, when simply because of a handicap, individuals were confined by misunderstanding, perception, shame, and fear. Due to no fault of their own, during this time tens of thousands were locked away, shielded from public view, and all but erased from everyday life.

Astrid Wagenschutz spent much of her youth with the people others ignored and dismissed. Born in Germany in 1920, the outgoing youngster lived in Norway for a decade and might have stayed there if her father had not made a trip to the United States to study the way the country was educating those viewed as mentally disabled. The America he discovered amazed and inspired him. It was a place of excitement, action, freedom, and energy. It was filled with thinkers and doers. It was a nation that opened its arms to those seeking second chances. It was very much the land of opportunity. Overcome with enthusiasm, and the offer of a teaching position at the University of Michigan, he gathered his family and immigrated to Ann Arbor. A year later, he moved to the Detroit area to oversee and teach at a facility housing and educating the mentally impaired. It was behind the walls of the Wayne County Training School, located between Northville and Plymouth, that Astrid, or Oz, as her friends called her, grew up.

Oz was an athletic, curious girl who loved to explore the grounds of the institution and the rural world beyond its walls. Living with her family in a dormitory, she exited the gates on a daily basis to play with friends, go to school, and run errands. Thanks to her father having solid employment, on the surface hers was a carefree life. Yet as she grew, she became acutely aware that the children who lived at the facility didn't have the same opportunities that she did. They didn't have parents who read to them, took them on outings, or planned birthday parties. Worse yet, no matter how loving these children were, society wasn't ready for them to live in a "normal" world. They were forgotten, and therefore their potential was stunted.

Perhaps having been born with poor vision caused the young American transplant to focus more on the plight of those around her than even most of the institution's staff. While fully understanding the children's limitations, Oz felt great empathy for their plight. Influenced by the way she relished the sights and sounds of the countryside, the manner in which she was intrigued by the scenes of nature playing out just outside the institution and how much she loved the freedom of being considered normal, she felt sorry for those living behind the walls who were unable to share in those special elements of life.

Thus, *handicapped* became a word that, when spoken, evoked great empathy and deep sadness for the immigrant child.

When she wasn't at school or exploring the world around Plymouth, Oz buried herself in books. It was reading that gave her an opportunity to expand her world into places others had never heard of and to experience adventures most of her friends couldn't imagine. As she grew, Oz vowed to someday explore as much of the world as she could. Even while living behind walls that clearly spelled out the limitations of its wards, she vowed to be limited by nothing.

At a time when women often married before graduating from high school, it was an anxious and excited Oz who left her small hometown to attend the University of Michigan. While there, pushing her mind to its fullest, she met the man she would fall in love with and marry. After his graduation, the couple settled into what was the American norm for married couples. He went into the construction business, she got a position in the insurance field, and three children were born. And every chance they got, with Robert, Elise, and Richard in tow, they lived Oz's dream by exploring the sights and wonders of America. Through thick glasses she took in vistas and watched performances and viewed treasured pieces of art, and she fully embraced each moment. Hers was a life lived without walls or barriers.

As the Great Depression gave way to World War II and then moved into the 1950s, Oz made sure there were no walls built around her children. Just as she had while growing up in the institution, she wanted her offspring to explore and grow. The mother constantly emphasized the greatest element of life was unwrapping the new wonders found along each step of the way. The message was not to get trapped by physical barriers and not to let others' perceptions of your potential keep you from living a full and rich life.

In a sense, Oz's idyllic world was the gift that her father sensed could be found in America. When he brought his family to the United States, it was in hopes that each of them would reap the multitude of opportunities he saw on his initial visit. Oz had experienced all that and more, and as she entered middle age, she was looking for even greater experiences. In 1961, seeking new adventures, the family moved to Arizona. Two years later, with little warning, the love of Oz's life was felled by disease. Within a month, her husband was totally disabled, and it would rest upon her to take care of him and find a way to pay the bills. Thus, she was now the family's sole provider, and her world was suddenly made smaller because of her husband's limitations. It would stay that way until he died. Then, at seventy, when she was once more traveling and exploring the world, her life turned upside down again. This time it was her own health that began to build seemingly impenetrable walls.

Though she'd never had normal eyesight, with glasses, Oz had been fully able to see everything around her. Now that was suddenly and dramatically changing. Not only were things not in sharp focus but shadows were pushing out the light. Her physician defined the problem as macular degeneration. Simply put, her vision was fading. Each week it grew a bit worse. In time, everything around her was out of focus, and she was relying on instinct and memory even more than her limited vision. Month by month and brick by brick, the disease built more walls around her world. For Oz, who had spent her life relishing each new sound and sight and living one adventure after another, her world was now almost claustrophobic. She was becoming just like the children she'd grown up around at the institution. Circumstances beyond her control were placing limits on what she could do and where she could go. She was trapped and dependent on others for things she once took for granted. Worse yet, people now perceived her differently. She was a woman to be helped and even pitied. It seemed the curious woman's rich life was behind her, and all that remained was counting down the days until the end. Unable to be fully independent and not satisfied to live with only her memories to keep her company, she moved to California to be near her daughter, hoping that in this new location she might find a way to regain some kind of independence. While she enjoyed being around her family, the city of Tulare offered her few chances to explore. It was not set up for someone with her problems.

By her eightieth birthday, frustration had set in. Oz was a walker. It was her nature to constantly keep moving, but now she had no depth perception and very limited forward vision. So although she had the physical health and endurance of a woman a generation younger, her failing eyesight was causing her to trip and fall on curbs and uneven sidewalks. Still, even though she was often bruised and battered by the experience, she continued to do her own shopping until the day she walked headfirst into a metal sign. Bleeding and a bit angry, she crept along, moving cautiously back to her home. It seemed that her blindness now gave her no options other than to spend her life trapped inside walls.

While the world was writing her off, a stubborn Oz,

not ready to give up, did some research. She discovered there were thousands of blind people in her state being guided by dogs. She had known about service dogs for years, but she had never considered what one could do for her. Could the dogs that were taking kids to college and adults to work also fit into her world? Conventional logic screamed out no. After all, she had no experience with dogs and had never even had one as a pet. And this was a minor issue when compared to her age. Oz was eighty-two. She was at a point in her life when most believed she no longer had the physical skills needed to work with a guide dog. So now she was not only battling the perceptions created by her blindness but also facing a growing problem in American society—age discrimination. People doubted her because they considered her too old. So would anyone give her a chance to knock down the walls that were now completely limiting her life?

Guide Dogs for the Blind offered Oz some hope when they agreed to meet with her. Representatives from the school came to her home, did an interview, and put her through a series of tests to evaluate her abilities to use and take care of a dog. They also asked her why she wanted a canine companion and how she planned on using her guide. Once the representatives got a feel for her specific needs, they spelled out what she would have to do to obtain a dog. It was not going to be a cakewalk. They were not going to cut her any slack because of her age. She would have to go through the same training as younger candidates. She would have to leave home; stay on their campus in Boring, Oregon; and be willing and able to do a lot of walking. As they described the physical toll the experience would take, it seemed as if they were almost trying to dampen her resolve. Yet, as walking was a part of her Norwegian heritage and she wanted to try to knock down the walls her blindness had built around her life, she was more than willing to make any and every sacrifice. In her mind, she had nothing to lose and everything to gain. With a smile, she all but told them to "bring it on."

As she counted down the days until her trip to Oregon, Oz's apprehension grew. This was something brand-new to her. She had no parameters on which to draw. Yet her fears could not cancel her resolve. Just like her father had left behind everything to come to the United States just because he believed the move would allow him to give his family something better, Oz knew that a dog was the only option she had to escape a life that lacked adventure. She wanted once more to be that little girl from Michigan who walked out the gate and explored fresh new places.

As Oz walked into the training school, she, like the

others of all ages around her, had no idea the promise
offered by this marriage of dog and human. Their hopes
were tempered by a natural tendency to limit the animal's potential. Each was falling into the same trap that
had once caused society to lock those who were mentally challenged behind walls. Yet in the first meeting
with the gentle yellow Labrador assigned to her, as it
leaned its body against her and stood confidently ready
to lead the woman into the world, Oz felt she could
overcome any obstacle placed in her path. And though
those first few steps were not steady or graceful, she
immediately sensed an independence she had all but
forgotten.

Oz's dog was named Riddler. From the moment
they first met, he was more than willing to lead, but it
took a while for Oz to fully trust him to be her guide.
Naturally, like most of those placed in this new position, she wanted to be in charge, to lead him rather
than allow him to do his job. Yet as the woman and
dog bonded, and as Oz learned how to use the harness
and the commands needed for the dog to work with her,
she found herself moving at a pace she hadn't achieved
in more than a decade. With each new session, there
was more bounce in her step and confidence in her
gate, and, within days, she had no fear of tripping on a
curb or running into a stop sign.

Like every student working with a dog, Oz was given the task of navigating Boring by herself at night. An instructor dropped her and Riddler off, and they were forced to rely on teamwork to return to the school. This was a final exam, and neither of them was going back to California until it was completed. Suddenly being alone with the dog offered a challenge unlike any she had ever known. There was no one to ask for help and no way of knowing which direction was which. As Oz listened to the sounds of night, as she gathered her wits and focused on the task at hand, she realized that for the first time in years she didn't feel like a vision-impaired senior citizen. She was that little girl exploring every path and meadow in and around Plymouth, Michigan. And though she didn't know where she was at this moment, she was free! As she ordered Riddler to move forward, it was as if Joshua was once more blowing his horn and the walls were coming down. Using her senses and trusting the dog's training, she passed the final exam with flying colors.

As wonderful as the experience at the school had been, it was when Oz returned home to Tulare, California, that her life really opened up. The uneven sidewalks that had once brought her to her knees were no longer a challenge, getting to the bus stop was easy, and trips to stores were a breeze. As the weeks went by, she grew in courage and fortitude; and with Riddler leading the way, she pushed farther into her community. She went to programs, club meetings, and social outings. She joined a gym and started to work out. Her world was bigger than it had been in decades, and like a road map, it just kept unfolding. As an added bonus, people's curiosity about the beautiful dog presented her with opportunities to make new friends and provided outlets for growth. Yet maybe the best part of her guide-dog experience took place behind the walls of her home.

Riddler quickly became more than Oz's eyes; he became her friend. When the harness was off, the dog exhibited loyalty and devotion unlike any she'd ever known from her family. He was her companion and confidant. As a deep love between the two bloomed, so did an even deeper layer of trust. When she laid her hand on his broad head and the Lab's wagging tail gently tapped her leg, Oz realized that as Riddler had reopened the world, he had been given a great gift as well. He was serving a purpose and living for the greater good. He seemed to understand that, too. He simply thrived on his service to her.

Riddler guided Oz for seven years. During that time, the two were inseparable. When his step finally slowed, he was retired and became the family pet for her grandchildren. Though it was tough not to have the incredible dog in her home, the woman found another set of eyes in the form of a black Lab named Eddie. The new arrival was more laid-back but every bit as loyal.

Eddie's training and adaptive nature allowed Oz to keep her independence well into her nineties. He accompanied her to the hospital for two hip replacements and got her up on her feet again to make sure she completed her therapy. Their hearts all but beat as one, as together, one step after another, they faced Oz's challenges of both blindness and advancing age. And when the woman decided it was time to go into an assisted living facility, the dog went with her.

It took almost no time for Eddie to map out their new home, and within a few weeks, he also discovered a new calling. With no guidance, the Lab stepped beyond his training and became the facility's morale director. When he wasn't guiding Oz, he somehow sensed when residents were depressed or lonely and spent time with them. This time the wall being broken down by the guide dog gave lonely souls something to look forward to each day—a wagging tail and a head to pat. Eddie grew into the new role of joyful guide and companion to those who had all but given up on life. He was the brightest spot in the day and the sunshine behind the wall. He was the reason many still wanted to live!

While visiting a neighbor, Oz fell on a patio. She broke her pelvis and several ribs and split open her head. As her host had recently left on an errand, she and Eddie were completely alone. With blood gushing from her wound, the dog jumped to the rescue. Barking at the top of his lungs, he alerted everyone within a hundred yards that something was amiss. If he hadn't voiced his concerns, Oz would have bled to death. He then frantically waited for more than a month for her to heal and work her way back to health in a rehab center. As much for her dog as for herself, Oz pushed herself to the limit so that Eddie could once more return to what he loved to do.

As Oz and Eddie embark on their new adventures, the woman has come full circle. What she knows now, she wished she could have appreciated while growing up at the institution for the mentally impaired. Everyone—no matter their visible limitations—has potential. They just need the opportunity to grow and explore. If they can't do it on their own, then they need a guide to move beyond the walls. And sometimes the best guides are those that never judge and show approval with a wagging tail.

Down but Not Out

Determination gives you the resolve to keep going in spite of the roadblocks that lay before you.

Denis Waitley

There is a claustrophobic fear that accompanies paralysis. That fear goes beyond not being able to defend yourself; it digs deep into your mind and screams that there is no longer a place for you in the world. The isolation of being so different brings on unimaginable loneliness.

The small raft was slowly drifting out toward the middle of Lake Powell. Within minutes it would be so far from shore its owners would have to secure a boat to retrieve it. As sixteen-year-old Tim Daynes watched the small vessel continue its uncharted journey across the waves, his friends debated about what to do. As he continued to silently study the scene, Tim sensed the wind picking up and the raft moving more quickly toward the open water. The raft was not his, so he had little stake in this small life episode. Whether he acted or not, someone would eventually get the raft back. But, as he had been a competitive swimmer for most of his life, his retrieving it would seem to be the easiest option. Besides, it was in his nature to do good deeds for others. He had always been that way. He was the kid who would carry in groceries or mow a family friend's yard. So here was the opportunity for him once more to do a selfless favor for someone else.

Standing in waist-deep water, he took a few steps forward. As was usually the case, the lake floor edged down a bit, and the warm water rose against his body. A few more feet and he would likely be in over his head. Turning, he waved back to his friends, tossed off a big smile, took a deep breath, and executed a perfect racing-style dive into the water. It was a move he'd done a hundred times, with many of those dives performed in Lake Powell. Yet this time things went horribly wrong. Just in front of him, hidden by water reflecting the bright sun, was a sandbar. He met the obstruction head first with the entire momentum of his powerful action compressing his neck and shoulders. For a moment he was stunned. A few seconds later, when his head cleared, he realized it was time to act and get to the surface, but his body wouldn't comply. It was as if he were glued to the bottom.

Logic told him his life was now measured in seconds. As time slowed to a crawl, Tim's brain screamed at his arms and legs to move, but the athletic body that had never failed him now seemed deaf to his urgings. He was completely helpless, and his breath was slowly giving out. His lungs began to ache, and his mind was caught in a web of both panic and acceptance. During those moments, the irony of facing death by drowning in chest-deep water did not escape him.

There is no way to scream for help when you are underwater. And when you can't move your arms, there is no way to signal that you are in trouble. As Tim attempted to will his body back into action, he wondered if those on the beach were watching for him to surface. If he couldn't manage to move, how long would it be before one of them sounded the alarm and raced out to find him?

As one minute became two and the last of his breath drained from his lungs, Tim heard muffled voices followed by the sound of bodies rushing through the water. At that same instant, he broke free of the sand and somehow bobbed to the surface. Someone reached him a few seconds later and turned him over. As they did, he grabbed what was at that time the most precious thing in the world—a mouthful of air.

There is something about being so close to death that makes you deeply appreciate everything, including the bright sun shining into your eyes and the breeze on your cheek. Tim was alive, and for a few moments, that was all that mattered. Then the horror of not being able to move flooded his senses. Something was very wrong, he was sure of that; but as he grabbed another grasp of sweet oxygen, he figured that when the shock subsided, movement would return. He just had to wait a little longer.

The world that Tim could see but could no longer touch seemed blanketed in a strange fog. It was as if he was somehow no longer a part of it. He could see the concerned expressions on his friends' faces and could even hear their prayers, but he could no longer connect with them. Those who had rescued the young man quickly assessed that while he had been saved from drowning, Tim still had some serious issues. When they brought him out of the water and onto the shore, and it was discovered he couldn't move, an ambulance was called. After what seemed like an eternity, a team of EMTs stabilized his vitals, assessed his issues, and made their report. After an ambulance ride, the East Salt Lake High School junior was evaluated at the local hospital, where the full depth of problems was revealed. Unable to properly treat such horrific injuries at Lake Powell, a helicopter was summoned, and Tim was flown to the University of Utah Medical Center.

A long helicopter flight was followed by more tests. His mother and father were then called in and given the grim news. Their son had broken both the C-3 and C-4 vertebrae. If he managed to avoid an infection or pneumonia and live through the next few days, the best the family could hope for was that Tim would spend his life as a quadriplegic. In fact, his injuries were so severe it was doubtful that he would ever be able to even feed himself again.

The news was devastating. In an instant, a healthy, athletic teenager was facing a life without movement and at the moment was fighting just to live. Unable to breathe on his own, he had been placed on a ventilator. When he was finally stabilized, the surgeons inserted a metal plate into his neck. Then came even more bad news. The accident had not only left Tim unable to move from the neck down but also left him unable to speak. It was sobering to consider a vital, young teen unable to move or talk, but for the time the goal had to be keeping him alive.

If Tim had not been so strong, he likely would have died during his first month in the medical center. Several times his lungs collapsed and his vitals coded. It seemed that he was being revived from the dead about as often as his lungs were being suctioned out. He was constantly on the edge between life and death.

Though praying for a miracle, Tim's parents and brother and sister readied themselves for a funeral that they were told would surely happen soon. The young man they so dearly loved—the one with the wicked sense of humor and cutting wit—was fighting a battle he couldn't possibly win. When his weight dropped to eighty-five pounds, it seemed the end was drawing near. Yet amazingly Tim kept fighting. After several months, his voice came back, as did very slight movement in his arms. Along with those positive signs, his appetite returned. Finally, more than six months after he had made the dive that so severely changed his life, Tim was dismissed from the hospital. It was the answer to his family's prayers, but it also offered them another major hurdle. The Daynes' home was simply not equipped for a person who could not walk. As Tim moved back into his bedroom, a team went to work remodeling the house. As the world around him was turned into a place where a quadriplegic could function, the boy worked on creating his own miracle. He was determined to do the impossible and walk again.

Physical therapy gave him some strength back. In time he was able to sit in a wheelchair and even move it forward with his arms, but his fingers would not work and his legs were useless. That meant having to adapt to special tools that allowed him to feed himself as well as realizing that if he dropped something, he would have to ask someone to pick it up. He was completely dependent on others.

As he slowly learned to adapt to his new normal, he was confronted with something he hadn't anticipated. His friends were uncomfortable with him. Though they visited when he first arrived home, in time, they found excuses not to come over. In their minds, the young man they had loved was gone. So the teen's next battle would be convincing those around him that while he couldn't move, he was still the same person.

After making up a half a year's worth of classes, he returned to school determined to graduate with his class. This meant learning more new skills and dealing with a building that was not set up for a kid in a wheelchair. Sensing the best way to handle things

Tim Daynes with his first service dog, Yaz.

was with humor, Tim poked fun at himself in a fashion that he hoped would ease people's sense of discomfort. To further push himself out into the public eye and convince his friends he was still the same kid, he ran for class vice president using the slogan "Roll with Tim." He won that election, but still, his world was a lonely one. Not many teenagers had time to include someone with a severe disability in their activities. His life was therefore little more than school and home.

In 1991, after graduation and as he prepared to find a way to attend college, Tim saw a picture of a dog standing with its front feet beside a cash register while holding a wallet in his mouth. The caption explained that the animal was trained to do everything from pulling its owner's wheelchair to giving a store clerk a credit card to pay for goods and services. This seemed to be the answer for Tim's desire to reclaim some independence. With a service dog assisting him with all things others took for granted, he might even be able to go to college. A few telephone calls connected him with Canine Companions for Independence. As he nervously explained his situation, he prayed the organization would not be overwhelmed with his seemingly insurmountable needs.

By training a canine partner to do the things people with disabilities could no longer do for themselves, for more than a generation, Canine Companions had been helping people much like Tim live a full life. During that time, thousands of dogs had been placed, and as many people had regained some of their independence. Once Canine Companions understood Tim's needs, they went to work finding and training a dog that could help the young man reach and even surpass his goals. Yet this marriage of dog and man would not happen overnight. For Tim, who wanted everything to happen *now*, this wait would be a test in patience. It would also mean more months he would have to look to those around him to complete even the most trivial of chores.

It would be a full year before Canine Companions called with the good news that they had found the right match for Tim. Now it was time for two intense weeks of bonding and training at the school's California center.

Yaz was a huge yellow Lab. He was the canine equivalent of a plow horse. Unlike a thoroughbred born to run, he was a plodder. He moved methodically, with precision and power. As the two bonded and learned to work together, Yaz's focused personality also came into play. Yaz had a servant's heart, and fulfilling Tim's needs brought him obvious joy. Pulling his wheelchair, opening a door, picking up a book, or paying for an item at a store seemed to be more than just jobs to Yaz; they were acts of compassion. It was as if the dog lived for those moments! As the training moved forward and Tim began to understand the walls the dog was capable of breaking down, the young man was overwhelmed. Yaz was a life-changer, and his potential seemed unlimited! Tim could hardly wait to show off his skills to his family.

After graduating from the training school, it was time to get back on the University of Utah campus where the dog's real impact would be felt. In the past, Tim had been on an island. Most were uncomfortable approaching or talking to him. So the injury had done more than take away his ability to move; it had also isolated him from most of society.

Tim understood the reasons those around him were intimidated. They were scared that they would ask the wrong question or say something that would hurt his feelings. Unlike high school where the same people were around him all day, in college, connections were liquid. During the day he rarely saw anyone more than once, and few of those meetings led to meaningful conversation. So in midst of a social world, it was easy to be awash in loneliness. Hence, the paralysis not only had taken away much of who he had been but also had affected Tim's perception of his place in the world. Because of people's reactions to his condition, he stayed home as much as possible. But Yaz's curious nature, stamina, and desire to work forced a change of the college student's point of view.

As the big yellow Lab led Tim to his classes, those who had once avoided him now rushed up to meet him. Complete strangers even searched for ways to start conversations. It seemed that everyone wanted to know all about Yaz and what he did for Tim. As he explained the dog's specialized training, the strangers quit being strangers and became friends. Many told him about their pets, and some began to feel so comfortable they asked Tim to explain what had happened to him. Suddenly, the world was not nearly as intimidating as it had been.

Back in his apartment, there was something much deeper going on. Not being able to move is tough. It weighs on the spirit as much as it does the body. It brings with it a depression that can cripple the mind. This happens most often when the person with a disability is alone. Beyond the dozens of commands needed to meet Tim's physical needs, Yaz had also been trained to be a companion. He had earned his place at Tim's side because he could pick up on mood changes as easily as he could open a door or bring the man a telephone. When Yaz sensed the gloom creeping in, he'd grab one of his toys and demand Tim play with him, or he would find a way to get the young man out of the house. This led to exploring new areas of campus and participating in events Tim would have never considered attending in the past. In these experiences new opportunities for relationships opened up.

As Tim and Yaz made new friends, they were invited to the student center for coffee. That led to invitations to social outings. In these casual settings, with the dog at his side and new friends talking about everything from basketball to the latest movies, Tim's wit, charm, and positive attitude had an opportunity to shine. His spirits were soaring.

Once people were given the chance to look beyond the wheelchair, they found they had a great deal in common with the young man. And Tim's companionship offered a bonus that no one else on campus could match. Being his friend meant you had a chance to pet Yaz's big head. So a relationship with Tim was a two-for-one deal.

As the negatives in his life became positives, as he discovered that people could appreciate him and even love him in spite of his disability, Tim began to challenge himself. He was no longer content just to get a degree; he was going to find new ways to expand his world. He got involved in wheelchair sports, and, in 1996, with Yaz leading the way, Tim carried the Olympic torch. In the span of a few months, Tim's life had gone from being empty to being so full he had trouble fitting everything into his calendar. And just when it seemed things could not get any better, they did.

Nurses regularly came by Tim's apartment to help him with needs that even Yaz wasn't trained to do. One of these visitors stirred emotions that Tim had figured would never be a part of his life. Every time he was around Karen, the young man's heartbeat accelerated. Initially, as he studied the woman, he thought, If only I wasn't paralyzed, I would ask her out. In the past the "if only" thoughts would have won out. He would not have had the confidence to suggest a movie or dinner. Yet Yaz had brought something completely unexpected into his life. He accepted Tim and saw his potential. It was also the dog who pushed "if only" from the man's college experience. Because of Yaz, he went everywhere and did almost anything. Could that self-confidence and value be extended beyond school and into the realms of love? The look on Yaz's face when Karen visited seemed to say, "Go for it!" Willing up all his courage, Tim asked the nurse out on a date, and she shocked him by accepting. Within weeks Tim discovered, that just like Yaz, the nurse saw beyond the wheelchair and into his heart.

As the big yellow Lab rebuilt Tim's life and paved the way for love, it seemed only natural for Yaz to be the ring bearer at Tim and Karen's wedding. Surrounded by scores of friends, embracing the most incredible celebration of acceptance he had ever known, Tim was able to say, "I do," because of what a dog had done.

The best moment in Tim's life was the day Yaz walked into it. The worse moment was when Yaz was felled by an infection. Tim was with the Lab as he breathed his last. After he said farewell to his old friend, the brokenhearted young man wheeled himself from the room, swearing he would never have another dog.

When Canine Companions presented Tim with Yaz, he was near the lowest point of his life. As the dog helped him gain independence, Tim was lifted out of despair and given a second chance at life. Now he had Karen to depend upon, so it seemed a service dog was not as necessary as it had been five years before. He figured he could get by without one. Besides, there could never be another Yaz; he was one of a kind, and it was time to move on. With time he figured that his broken heart would find a way to heal. Yet as the weeks became months, as Tim went back to work and plunged into his life, he discovered that loneliness and grief created their own kind of paralysis. He could no longer ignore the fact there was still a huge hole in life that nothing could fill. Worse yet, without Yaz leading the way, the old pattern of people avoiding the man in the wheelchair resurfaced. During those lonely days, Tim realized once more the dog had been more than just a servant and best friend; he had been the icebreaker needed to build new relationships. Thus, though initially it felt as if he was showing disrespect to Yaz and all that he had brought to his life, Tim again connected with Canine Companions and asked for another dog.

The organization once more examined Tim and where he was in life. Their study led to them picking out a different type dog. Ehreth was a golden retriever and yellow Lab mix who was smaller and more energetic than Yaz. Why the change? Because Tim's life had changed. He was now married, so the dog's role would be a bit different.

Ehreth was with Tim when he opted to go back to school and earn his master's degree in social work. In fact, the University of Utah saw to it that Ehreth wore a cap and gown just like Tim's at the graduation ceremony. The dog would also be by the man's side when he began his new job as a vocational counselor. And for the next seven years, Ehreth would open the doors to countless professional and personal relationships.

The impact of dogs didn't stop there; Sakai and Irish followed. Sakai was a black Lab/golden cross whose athleticism pushed Tim to become even more active in sports, while Irish took the young man on incredible trips to places most people only dream about. So each dog, using its own special gifts, dramatically influenced and expanded Tim's world.

When he speaks to groups, Tim says, "When you're going through a difficult transition trying to accept being disabled and you have a dog trained to be there for you, you have a wonderful relationship with the dog helping you. My first service dog, Yaz, gave me confidence and something to talk about. These service dogs are amazing, spiritual gifts from God. I think Canine Companions deserves applause for what they've been able to do with these magnificent animals. They've made me a much better person."

More than two and a half decades after having Yaz come into his life, Tim is a happily married, successful professional who has traveled all over the world. Through his work, he has helped hundreds of damaged people rebuild their lives; through his life, he has been an inspiration to even more. And by his side, each step of the way has been a dog trained specifically for his ever-changing needs.

When Tim Daynes was injured, he was using his swimming skills to help with what looked like a very simple act of service. For twenty-five years, Tim's life has been enhanced, impacted, and dramatically changed by four dogs that have proved there are no simple acts of service. Each one makes a mighty effect in helping those who are down to again rise up.

A Ticket to Ride

My motto in life is take risks; you don't have a voice if you don't. You have to venture outside your boundaries. That's what life is all about.

Kelly Wearstler

You don't have to view the road in front of you to have the vision to see the potential of those around you. But to travel that road and share your vision, you must have a guide.

George Kerscher was born in 1950 and raised in inner-city Chicago. He grew up close to Wrigley Field and, on summer days, rode his bicycle to the home of the Cubs. With an awestruck gaze, he watched as many future Hall of Famers strolled in and out of the fabled ballpark. He got the chance to see those same baseball heroes in action by helping clean up the stadium after games. His hours of picking up old programs, empty drink cups, and peanut bags earned him a ticket to the game the following day. From his bleacher seats he watched hometown superstars such as Ernie Banks and Ron Santo as well as visiting all-stars such as Stan Musial, Willie Mays, and Hank Aaron. For the budding athlete, seeing scores of National League baseball games flooded youthful dreams with thousands of unforgettable memories.

When it wasn't taking him to Wrigley Field or school, George's bike carried the boy to almost every part of the city. During these trips, he saw people who had moved to Illinois from all over the world and listened to them speak a dozen different languages. Through their stories, dress, and lifestyles, he gained a deep appreciation of different cultures as well as a thirst to see the width and breadth of the world with his own eyes.

In his youthful explorations of the Windy City, George also witnessed the plight of those suffering with disabilities. Because of birth, accidents, or war, these people had been marginalized and pushed aside. For them, pity was an everyday facet of life, and the struggle just to survive was a monumental challenge.

In a city that fueled passions and dreams, these folks were denied both.

At home the boy was surrounded by love and constantly encouraged to use his God-given talents. George's father was one of the many in Chicago still practicing an old-world skill. As a sausage maker for Oscar Mayer, he was a man of great imagination. Each day, using a huge array of spices, the family patriarch created new recipes for the company's meats. The best of his work was tested on management. If approved, the blends ended up wearing the Oscar Mayer label and were sold in stores all around the globe. Although George never followed in his father's footsteps, he did inherit the man's great creativity. Yet when he graduated from high school, his intelligence and curiosity took a backseat to his athletic talent.

After fielding offers from several universities, in the late summer of 1968, the young man left the Windy City and moved to Wichita, Kansas. In the middle of the Wheat Belt, George put on pads and hit the gridiron. He quickly discovered that playing football for Wichita State University didn't offer the same thrills he had experienced in high school ball. Even though his coaches, teammates, friends, and family urged him to stay in Kansas, after a year, he returned home. This change of direction would save his life.

On October 2, 1970, an airplane carrying the Wichita State defensive squad football team crashed in the Colorado mountains, killing most on board.

A shaken George mourned the loss of friends as he continued his education first at Benedictine College, then at Wright Junior College and the Chicago Circle Campus of the University of Illinois. Struggling to focus on a career plan, he finally graduated with a major in education at Northeastern Illinois University. Armed with a degree, he was ready to challenge the world, but an unexpected development put his career on hold.

In the last few months of college, George noted that his field of vision was shrinking. He mentioned it during a routine physical, which paved the way for him to meet with a vision specialist. Tests revealed the unimaginable; the young man had retinitis pigmentosa (RP). With great sadness the physician informed his patient that RP was an incurable disease that would steal his eyesight within five to ten years. At a time when most were focusing on career options, George cashed in his savings in order to have a chance to see the lands he had heard about during his youthful bicycle trips through various Chicago neighborhoods. If he didn't see those places now, he knew he never would.

Through an always appreciative gaze and with
a sense of desperation, George took in the sights of
Paris, London, and Berlin. As he walked through art
museums and stood on mountaintops, he did his best
to deeply imprint each new view into the innermost
recesses of his mind. He pushed himself to study
detail, color, and contrast, to memorize what others
hurriedly viewed as if this would be the last time he
would ever see the Eiffel Tower, London Bridge, or
snow-covered Alps.

After returning to the United States, he employed
the same tactic as he walked through his hometown,
carefully observing the waves crashing on the shores
of Lake Michigan, the shoppers rushing down the
Million Dollar Mile, and even the humble hotdog
vendors whose carts could seemingly be found on
every corner. Even in the friendly confines of Wrigley
Field, a place he knew so well from his many visits as
a youth, George studied every seat, rafter, and brick.
Just like the Chicago icon Ernie Banks, who was now
in the twilight of his long career, the young man's sight
would soon be playing out as well, and neither the
baseball star nor the recent college grad took the visual gifts they were now seeing for granted. There
would be no second chances. These were moments
that had to be treasured for as long as possible.

Though failing a bit more each day, his eyes were still functioning well enough to spot and know beauty. He had known Gail for some time. They had shared many adventures together. She knew his condition and accepted it. So it was no surprise when the recent nursing graduate returned George's love. With his new bride in tow, he left the United States once more. This time it was to explore the wilds of Canada while teaching special education at the Buffalo Narrows School District in Saskatchewan. A few years later, as he and his wife welcomed their own children into their world, the couple moved to Stevensville, Montana. While maintaining his home in the mountains and forests around Darby, George took a position as a teacher of English and transitioned into the manager of the computer lab. He relished his new job and his students so much that he didn't even mind the forty-mile daily commute; though, when the opportunity came up, George took a job at Stevensville. When the weather was pretty, he reverted to his youthful habit of riding his bike the ten miles to work. On these trips, seeing the picturesque landscape gave him a chance to imprint even more unforgettable images into his mind.

Falling in love with the emerging field of computer science, George wrote a grade book program for his fellow educators. He also became one of the first teachers to instruct junior high and high schoolers how to write original programs using the logo language. Within a year of his arriving at Stevensville, his pupils knew more programming than many college graduates with computer science degrees.

When he brought in audio recordings of books and had his students follow the words on the pages in their print editions, this evolved into the idea of a computer doing the synchronizing of text and audio. At the time, this was a revolutionary concept. George noted that the kids who never read books grew to love literature when a computer read the text to them. Overnight their test scores and course understanding increased. Like an explorer searching for treasure, the teacher now had a passion to go where no educator had gone before. Each day, using his classroom as a laboratory, he pushed the learning envelope a bit further while building the foundation for a life of achievement.

While George was thriving in the challenges of expanding his rural pupils' cutting-edge skills in computer science, his vision loss began to accelerate. Soon he was forced to give up driving. Hitchhiking from his home to school in the early morning and then back each night is how he now commuted. His long treks became so well known in the area that he came to be good friends with most of those who picked him up along his way. Some even changed their schedules to give the outgoing, positive teacher a lift. For George, the experience pushed him to appreciate the way others were allowing him to keep a piece of his independence. Without them trusting and watching out for him, he would have been much like the disabled people he had seen as a child who struggled just to survive each new day.

While the hitchhiking added a couple of hours to his daily work schedule, it would not deter him from continuing to challenge his students. He thrived by getting the chance to expand their creativity and point of view. Yet when his eyesight grew so bad he could no longer read their papers, even with a magnifying glass, he was forced to leave something he dearly loved. Walking away from a career that he viewed as a calling, George wondered if he would ever have the chance to again make any kind of lasting impact.

Looking for a miracle, in 1985 George traveled to Boston to consult with the top experts in the field of RP. They sadly informed the thirty-five-year-old man that there was no hope. Not ready to become completely isolated from life and looking for a way to continue his career, he opted to go to graduate school. At that time there was no Americans with Disabilities Act, and thus he was going to have to qualify for school as any other person would. That meant passing the standard version of the Graduate Record Exam. As he took the test, a person read the questions to him. Although he knew he had knocked the top out of science and math, he didn't even attempt the history portion of the exam because of the essays required. Realizing he would not be accepted to school without confirmation of his knowledge in this discipline, he composed a letter suggesting his undergraduate English degree and history courses should serve as proof of his knowledge. After a few meetings, he won over those in charge of computer programming at the University of Montana and was allowed to enter school. He didn't get to celebrate for long. While his fellow students were buying books and checking class schedules, he was still facing a myriad of problems.

Most of the books he needed for his coursework were not accessible in audio form, thus he had to rely on assigned volunteer readers. He could study only when these volunteers were available to help him, which quickly became frustrating. Still he pushed ahead. When George met the author of a book on MS-DOS computer language, he asked if he could have the electronic files generated for the publication. This should have given him a way to "read" using his computer, but the results were completely unsatisfactory.

George Kerscher with the
indomitable Nesbit.

So, using the creativity he inherited from his sausage-maker father, he began to write a program to address his needs as a blind person. In just three weeks, he created the first digital version of a publication that could be read by anyone using assistive technology.

Word quickly spread through the blind community of George's breakthrough computer innovation. Others wanted the chance to use it. Sensing an opportunity, the grad student worked on a business model. Within a few months, Computerized Books for the Blind (CBFB), a nonprofit organization for the distribution of books in ASCII files on floppy disks, was born.

Microsoft Press was the first publisher to sign up, and others quickly joined. The university gave George an office, and with support from the school's Institute on Disability, he produced over 700 titles in three years. The man who had once believed his chance to make an impact might have ended with his teaching career was now opening up the world for thousands. He was even credited with coining a new educational term—*print disabled*—and in 1998 was even named the innovator of the year by *U.S. News and World Report*. That recognition led to a challenge George never believed he would have to face. He was receiving invitations to address conventions, speak to schools, and meet with others involved in opening the world of education and innovation for persons with disabilities. His first trip was to a higher educational conference in New Orleans. Armed with his cane, he took off. For the next decade, whenever he left his Montana home, it would be that cane that led him. But just like having people read his textbooks for him, traveling alone without eyes quickly grew frustrating.

It was on a trip to the East Coast when he met up with a blind colleague at a conference that his world changed. With a dog guiding them, the men had no problem navigating the complex hotel and convention center. They also easily found the elevators, restaurants, restrooms, and even trashcans. For the first time in years, George felt as if he was operating at a normal speed.

Once at home he contacted the leading guide-dog schools. Some felt that George's unique lifestyle would be too hard on a dog. They pointed out that he spent too much time on planes and in hotels. Others wondered if his constant traveling into urban areas while living in a rural setting in Montana might create issues for a service dog. It was Guide Dogs for the Blind in San Rafael, California, that finally gave him a shot. Little did the organization realize the dog they were to match with one of the country's best-known blind innovators would emerge in the new century as an industry star.

George spent February of 1999 in Class 591 at Guide Dogs for the Blind. He was partnered with a twenty-one-month-old yellow Labrador retriever named Nesbit. While no marriage of dog and human is ever seamless, George and Nesbit's bond came easily, as did their ability to work and move as one. When Gail visited her husband during the training, the dog immediately fell in love with the other member of the household too. Upon graduation, the Kerschers had no doubt that seeking a guide dog was going to greatly enhance their home lives. After all, Nesbit already seemed like he had always been a part of the family. Yet it would be during the first trip away from Montana that the dog's real value was displayed.

While Nesbit had been all but perfect in his guide duties at home, in the woods, and the city of Missoula, a meeting in Milwaukee, Wisconsin, offered him his first real test. As they left for their first trip, George was filled with excitement and a touch of apprehension, while the dog was calm and focused. What George quickly discovered was that the Lab was not just a guide; he was also going to improve the man's health. When using his cane, George often ran into things, which, from time to time, left bruises. With Nesbit leading the way through airports, along streets, and at the meetings, it was clear sailing. He also discovered that he didn't need to build in extra time in his schedule for travel. No longer was he edging along slowly; with the dog leading the way, the former college athlete was once again in the fast lane. Thanks to Nesbit, for the first time since he went blind, George moved with speed and grace.

That initial trip to Milwaukee revealed another benefit the man hadn't anticipated. Nesbit was an icebreaker. Because of the dog's professional skills coupled to his outgoing personality, people approached George. While his blindness had made him somewhat of a social outcast, Nesbit made the man the center of attention. On the plane, in restaurants, at his hotel, and at the meetings, the spotlight was always on the pair. Nesbit was the bridge George needed to have others fully relate to and value him as a professional. By their viewing him on equal terms as a businessman, he was given the opportunity to open the door for others who were vision impaired.

During this trip, the full value of trust between dog and a man was forged as well. At one point George asked Nesbit to go forward, but the dog balked. He tried it several more times, but the canine held its ground. Finally George discovered that if he had made a step forward he wouldn't have been on a level, safe floor, but heading down steep, slippery steps. From this moment on, if the dog didn't move, George didn't question Nesbit's judgment. Over the next nine years, this trust likely saved the man from injury on hundreds of occasions.

Now recognized as one of the world's foremost experts on communication and publication for those with visual impairments, George was traveling hundreds of thousands of miles a year. His trips took him not just to every corner of the United States but also to Europe and Asia. On most of these trips, Nesbit was by his side. In his role as a guide, the dog took George through the chaotic streets of Rome and scores of other cities. No matter the location or environment, the dog was never perturbed or distracted by the mass of humanity or the wall-to-wall traffic. Always focused on his mission, he got George to where he was going as well as kept him safe along the way. Once there, Nesbit became the magnet that drew people forward so that George could tell and demonstrate the abilities and potential of the blind.

When George was named the 2001 Dayton Forman Award cowinner for groundbreaking work on Digital Talking Books, Nesbit led the man onto the stage. The same was true in 2004 when George won the Harry J. Murphy Catalyst Award, a biennial award presented by the Trace Center to honor those who bring people together and facilitate the efforts of others in the field of technology and disability. The dog was by his side in 2005 when he was selected as the chair on one of the most important blind communication programs in the world, and in 2007 when the University of Montana awarded the businessman an honorary doctorate of humane letters. Nesbit was with him for scores of other honors and awards, and though it was George's groundbreaking work in developing tools for the blind that created these accolades, the man always gave the dog credit for being the most valuable player on the team. Ironically, the next year it would be the dog giving the man the credit.

In 2008, Delta Airlines recognized Nesbit as a "Million Miler." He thus became the first dog to reach that unique milestone. What this award really signified was not the world the dog has seen but the world the guide dog had opened up for the man. During those million miles, George had traveled around the globe educating, inspiring, and motivating countless people. Without Nesbit, all of those miles would have been much too difficult to travel, and many of those trips would have not been made. George knew his imprint was possible because he followed in Nesbit's footsteps.

Beyond his work as a guide and constant companion in George's travels, the dog also had the knack of remembering those the pair had met before. The vigorous wagging of Nesbit's tale was the sign an old friend was approaching. This unique trait meant George was warned when a business associate was headed his way. Thus, Nesbit being by his side gave the man time to be prepared to share the latest advances and innovations his company was offering and developing. It seemed the dog guided the businessman's every step while also serving as his social manager and top salesman. In other words, they were partners in business and life.

After almost nine years of service, Nesbit was elevated to being the family pet, and another Labrador, Mikey, took his place. Much like his forerunner, Mikey traveled more than a million miles, leading George not just around the globe but also into the White House to discuss issues concerning the blind. George was then appointed by President Obama to the board of the Institute of Museum and Library Services. When Mikey was forced into retirement, Kroner took over and now is the top dog.

Like almost all who have been led by a guide dog, George can point to various times when Nesbit, Mikey, and Kroner have literally saved his life by preventing a misstep or blocking him from danger. But more than being lifesavers, the trio of dogs has given George the same kind of independence he knew as a child riding his bike in Chicago and has allowed him to stimulate the minds of children with learning disabilities. His guides have allowed him to go to new places, meet fascinating people, experience the wonders of varied cultures, and share exciting educational and business innovations. Without the dogs, far fewer would have been able to meet the man and hear his remarkable story. So while no one can argue that George Kerscher is a man of great vision, it is the eyes of three dogs who have allowed him to bring that vision to the world.

Maintaining Balance

Man maintains his balance, poise, and sense of security only as he is moving forward.

Maxwell Maltz

When a person is prevented from moving forward and experiencing life, the world shrinks. A shrinking world steals hope and happiness. It robs a person of enthusiasm, brings on bitterness, and throws a life completely out of balance. Even if you require help, you must continue to move forward as well as look forward to regain your balance.

Even in the days of Vietnam War protests and social unrest, at a time when millions saw the military in a negative light, two recent high school graduates from completely different parts of the nation answered the call to serve their country. Scott was from Michigan and signed up with the US Navy while Philadelphia native Jenny opted for the Coast Guard. Their various duties took them around the globe, with Scott even serving in combat operations in the Far East. During those mosquito-filled moments, when snipers seemed to hide behind every tree and life always hung in the balance, all that mattered was living one more day. He had no idea that decades after his last tour in Vietnam and moving back into civilian life the war would come back to turn his world upside down.

After leaving the service in the mid-1970s, Scott and Jenny both attended college in Michigan. They met on campus and, after discovering how much they had in common, began dating. Songs such as "Lucy in the Sky with Diamonds," "You're No Good," "That's The Way (I Like It)," and "Let's Do It Again" provided a soundtrack to their days, and the two fell in love. With college degrees in hand, they married, so very anxious to start a life of their own.

Their occupations in the field of technology took them to Washington State. Living the American dream, they bought a home, became active church members, joined a few clubs, and started a family. Their friends described the Cawleys as having the hearts of servants. They gave their time, energy, love, and devotion to those who were forgotten, dismissed, misunderstood, or ignored. It seemed they never gave up on anyone. Their lives seemed to mirror that of the ideal 1950s and 1960s television families in every respect except one. Jenny and Scott's home had room for more than just their birth children; they also took in kids others had given up on. Over the next twenty years, eight children would come to call them Mom and Dad.

Though there were trials and challenges to having so many children in their lives, and though they had to give up many material possessions others around them took for granted, the Cawleys had such an optimistic outlook that it didn't seem to matter. They viewed their lifework as giving selfless love in order to build others up. Thus, they constantly took steps on faith. Time after time those steps were rewarded.

In 1995, in the midst of soccer matches and school events, in the middle of helping kids with homework and going to PTA meetings, a ghost from the past revisited the home and brought the outgoing, upbeat head of the household to his knees. Doctors determined the stroke that felled Scott was tied to his exposure to Agent Orange during his service in Vietnam. So while he had successfully dodged the bullets, mines, and bombs, another deadly product of that war had finally caught up with him. Suddenly the man, whose stamina and power were the envy of all the other fathers in the neighborhood, could not control the left side of his body. The stroke had also silenced Scott's booming voice and engaging laugh.

Any sports star who has ever been forced into physical therapy by a major injury will tell you that there is nothing harder than trying to work your way back to where you had been. Tasks that were once easy to do seem impossible, and progress is measured in small, painful steps. Those paralyzed by a stroke face even higher mountains. They are not dealing with just a knee or shoulder; they are trying to teach their minds to once more send messages to their arms and legs. The effort needed to even attempt this task requires Herculean sacrifice and fortitude. The recovery is often measured in years, if it can be measured at all.

With Jenny by his side and their children urging him on, Scott regained his voice. While his diction was no longer as clear or strong as it had once been, he could at least communicate. In time he also taught himself to walk again. But the doctors told him that he would never recover to the point where he could work or live independently. Essentially, without the help of those around him, he would remain homebound for the rest of his life.

Scott fully understood the diagnosis. He realized

that his once powerful body was now crippled in such a way his life would never be the same, but he wasn't going to give up on living. Putting on a happy face, he demanded that Jenny and the children not feel sorry for him or cater to him but rather put their own lives first. He would find a way to manage. Even as Jenny tried to look after his needs, Scott pushed her back into the world. He urged her to stay involved in church, clubs, and meetings. She needed to be with the kids during school programs. She had to continue to have time with her friends.

Jenny was able to support the family through her job as a medical technology sales representative, but that required her to be gone from home. When the kids were at school and she was at work, there was no one to help Scott. No matter the assurances he gave her about his ability to cope with any issues, she was worried. She was well aware that there were times when he would lose his balance, fall to the floor, and have to struggle just to pull himself up onto a chair. As the falls became more common, Jenny's concern grew. She needed help. As she searched for alternatives from changing jobs to finding someone for home health care, she was told of an Oregon woman who trained dogs for mobility service.

In 1999, Jenny made a call to Leslie Rappaport and

explained Scott's situation. A meeting followed. After evaluating the man's specific needs, Leslie returned to Kings Valley Collies and began working with a large, sable collie. Over the next few weeks, the trainer tried to duplicate the environment of the Cawleys' home and the various obstacles that were found in the area where the family lived. The dog was going to have to be comfortable with all types of public transportation, behave properly in social settings such as church and school, and keep its focus while being surrounded by active and loud children and a few curious cats.

Beyond dealing with the home and community, Lion, the collie Leslie felt was the perfect choice for this job, had to develop a sixth sense that went well beyond what was usually required of service dogs. Since the stroke, Scott was not always easy to understand. He also sometimes forgot words or got them out of order. So Lion was going to have to read his body language to know when Scott needed help getting out of a chair or was starting to lose his balance. This meant the trainer was going to need to simulate those situations as well. It took weeks of additional training to cover all the unique parameters of this particular case. Only when Leslie felt completely confident in the dog's ability did she bring Scott and Jenny to her training center and teach them what they needed to know to make this marriage of canine and human work.

Lion had no problem dealing with Scott's physical issues with balance. The dog was able to read, by the man's grip on the harness, if he needed to slow down or stop. When he sensed the man teetering on steps or struggling to get up from a chair, even if the wrong command was issued, Lion would lean into Scott to provide him support. Yet there was something else the dog quickly learned that escaped all human logic. Even before Scott felt the dizziness that caused him to lose his balance, the dog sensed it and pushed the man toward a chair. Lion's forecasting Scott's vertigo showed just how deeply the collie focused on his job, but how he was able to do this remained a mystery.

Within a month of placement, Lion had reopened the door to Scott's world. With the dog leading the way, the Vietnam vet was back in church, going out to eat with friends, and attending the kids' school activities. Lion even accompanied Scott on bus trips to the veterans' hospital. Jenny was able to relax for the first time in years, confident that when Scott was alone, the dog was there to meet his every need from bringing him a newspaper to retrieving a ringing phone.

Beyond the safety factor, Lion also provided companionship to a man who had been lonely and frustrated since his stroke. And because the dog saw him as a whole person rather than a damaged soul, Scott began to see himself that way as well. He was once more able to laugh and joke. He felt more comfortable around people. So while he still moved slowly and his steps were not as sure as they had been before the stroke, while he still at times searched for words, he carried himself with confidence once more.

When Scott was out in public, Lion changed perceptions in a way no human could. The collie was beautiful, almost Lassie-like in bearing, and folks wanted to get to know him. That meant countless people came up to speak to Scott. To adults it provided him with a line of communication, and to kids it made Scott cool. The pride that the man displayed when showing off Lion was the best medicine in the world.

Every service dog is unique, and when that dog is off harness, that personality really comes out. Leslie's choice of canine to match with Scott went beyond just filling the man's physical needs. The trainer knowingly picked a dog who would also bring laughter into the man's life.

Lion was a comedian. He had been that way as a pup. Off harness, he just loved to do things to make people laugh. He would sing along with the church choir, comment on television programs, and react to everything that happened at home. He found ways to aggravate the family's cats and tease the kids. During the day, likely with Scott's urging, he would find toys and hide them. Later, Lion and Scott would innocently watch as frustrated children turned the house upside down trying to find what the dog had hidden. When no one was looking, Lion would even steal wrapped Christmas presents. Day in and day out the dog found ways to keep things interesting, and that was as important to Scott as having Lion bring him physical stability.

When a death in the family forced the Cawleys to fly back East for a funeral, Lion was there to guide Scott safely through the airports. Over the coming weeks, as the family reflected on the loved one they had lost, the dog took on a new role; he found ways to comfort both Jenny and Scott.

Scott Cawley and Lion, who learned to predict Scott's medical needs.

Lion was also the key to the family being able to take vacations. With the dog watching over Scott, Jenny and the kids were able to go out on their own and see the sights without fear or guilt. If Scott wanted to leave the hotel room while they were gone to do a bit of beach walking or shopping on his own, Lion made sure the man's steps were safe. So while the dog had not been able to give Scott his old life back, Lion allowed the man to enjoy life and be secure in his new reality as well as provide the gift of independence for Jenny and the kids to fully embrace their lives and live their dreams.

Lion developed one more valuable and unexpected trait. People who have suffered a stroke like the one that felled Scott are easy prey. Thieves and bullies often take advantage of their disability. Somehow, the dog had no problem identifying trouble. When someone who seemed untrustworthy approached Scott, Lion kept his body between the intruder and his owner. No one was going to take advantage of Scott while Lion was on duty.

Lion served Scott for five years. When the big guy was felled by cancer, Leslie Rappaport trained a second collie to take his place. In 2004, Ramsey stepped up to the plate. This dog would face new challenges, one of which would require the ultimate sacrifice.

By the time Ramsey joined the family, Scott's condition was growing worse. His legs were now weaker, and he needed more help walking up ramps, stairs, and on uneven ground. Ramsey easily handled these chores. When Scott used a wheelchair, Ramsey was strong enough to pull the man where he needed to go. Yet it would take a major fall to prove the dog as a real lifesaver.

On a day when Jenny was out of town on business and the kids were at school, disaster struck. Scott was moving slowly through the house when he lost his balance. Though not on his harness, Ramsey was still carefully watching the man. Within a second of Scott's falling, the dog was by his side. After licking his face and receiving a weak pat on the head, the collie stepped back to assess the situation. Getting into the proper position, he poised himself to help Scott up, but the man was hurt too badly to move. Ramsey again paused and studied the scene before him. Somehow sensing he could not do what was needed, the dog ran to a table and retrieved the phone. He then brought it to the man and dropped it into his hand. Scott was just aware enough to make the emergency call. Within minutes a team was there to help. If it hadn't been for Ramsey's training and instincts, Scott would have been there for hours and might have even died.

With Scott's condition slowly deteriorating, each day offered new challenges. No longer was it just a phone or television remote that needed to be located and brought to the man; now it was a fork or spoon. Even during moments when Scott was not able to issue the right command, Ramsey somehow figured out what the man wanted. Thus, at a time when many in Scott's situation were being sent to a home for veterans, he was able to maintain a degree of independence while remaining with the family he so loved.

Ramsey was in his fifth year of service when the Cawleys took their four youngest children on a dream vacation to Disney World. The excitement of the July trip was immediately dampened when Jenny discovered there had been a mix-up on their hotel reservations. Unable to find rooms at any of the chains, the family opted for a cheaper motel along the beach. On the first morning, Jenny awoke before Scott and the kids and took Ramsey for a walk. Along the way she ran into folks she had met the night before. As she stood close to the water, the dog began to whine, pushing on the woman as if trying to get her to continue their walk. Jenny ignored the collie until finally Ramsey stepped around her and froze. Shocked by her normally well-behaved dog's rudeness, Jenny looked down to scold him and spied a coral snake. If Ramsey hadn't moved between her and the water, the most poisonous snake in the country would have likely bitten her. It was a now frightened Jenny who yanked the dog back from the water and hurried away from the snake. Once they were at a safe distance, one of her new acquaintances pointed out that the dog had just saved the woman's life. As she glanced to Ramsey, he shot back an expression indicating it was all in a day's work. But Jenny knew better; she and Scott now both owed their lives to the big collie.

Back in their hotel room, Jenny shared the high points of the morning walk with her family and amazed them with the story of Ramsey saving her life. To reward him for his service, the collie was given the morning off. As the Cawleys hurried off to breakfast, Ramsey seemed more than ready to catch up on sleep. An hour later when they returned, the dog was in the midst of a seizure. Though he had shown no reaction earlier, a hurried exam by the panicked family revealed the coral snake had bitten the collie. A veterinarian was quickly called in, but there was nothing that could be done. The snake's highly toxic venom was already crippling the canine's vital organs. Within an hour the dog was dead. The great irony was that while Ramsey had given his life in service to Scott, he had given up his life for Jenny.

The family's dream vacation was transformed into a nightmare. They had lost the dog whose skills had made this trip possible for Scott. Without Ramsey, the man's steps were once more unsure, and there was no way of forecasting when the vertigo would set in. As the family toured the amusement park and visited the city's other tourist meccas, their dependency on the dog became more and more obvious. Without Ramsey, all of them were lost.

When Jenny notified Leslie of the events leading to Ramsey's death, the trainer went back to work. She already had a large, handsome, sable collie that would fit the family's needs; but before she could give it to the Cawleys, the dog would have to learn how to read Scott's body language. In a very real sense this was like a college graduate going back to school to earn a master's degree. When the trainer was completely secure that Brynn knew his stuff, she invited Scott up for bonding and training.

Initially, Brynn served the family just as Lion and Ramsey had. He gave Scott a sense of independence and companionship, taking a load off Jenny's back, and played the role of family pet for the Cawleys' growing children. But in June of 2010, after less than a year on the job, the dog's role dramatically changed.

For fifteen years, Scott Cawley had battled a series of medical issues brought on by the Agent Orange he was exposed to while serving his country. Finally his body gave up the fight. The loss was devastating to Jenny and the children. Yet, just as Lion had first provided a light in Scott's dark world, Brynn's humor, energy, and compassion cut through their depression as well. As Jenny struggled to manage work and to raise the children, she would look at the dog and see a reflection of her husband's positive nature. It was as if a part of the man she loved was still there. And just as her husband had not wanted his illness to keep her from an active life, the dog who had served her husband wouldn't allow her to stay home either. Brynn wanted to get out of the house, and taking the dog out pushed Jenny back into the church, school functions, and outings with friends.

Three dogs served Scott Cawley. Lion provided him with a sense of independence and the will to live. Then Ramsey saved both his and his wife's life. Finally, Brynn embraced Scott's desire for his wife to have a full, rich life and pushed her back into the world rather than let her sink into depression. While it was Leslie Rappaport's training that provided the foundation for each of these collies' service, it was the dogs' ability to grow and to meet unexpected challenges that proved their real value. They provided the balance to keep those they served moving forward.

Hope

Hope is being able to see that there is light despite all of the darkness.

Desmond Tutu

Sometimes desperation can be the world's greatest crippler. It paralyzes our abilities to act, move, and take risks. It pushes us into the darkness and keeps us from seeking the light. To refind the light, we often need a guide—someone who knows where we want to go and has the courage to lead us there. Some guides are angels, but maybe there are others that walk on four legs and give those they touch the chance to fly.

Becky Peterson was a bright, outgoing, energetic teen. The pretty girl from Providence, Utah, was also vivacious, popular, and athletic. She set goals and worked to meet them. Hence, her friends thought of her as sweet but determined. A born optimist, she saw a future with unlimited possibilities and couldn't wait to experience as many of those exciting possibilities as imaginable. Yet she was also much more than an adventurous soul whose dreams were focused only on herself. She had not only depth and courage but also heart and was naturally empathetic. She sensed not just pain but potential. When people were down, she lifted them up. When others lacked confidence, she pointed out strengths. When Becky entered a room, she brought with her comfort, joy, and hope. The sparkle in her eyes could turn most frowns into smiles.

Growing up with loving parents and two older brothers, she was teased on occasion and took it in stride. She knew it was a way that her siblings showed love. When she was in high school, she was teased most often about her clumsiness. It seemed that in spite of her athletic gait and bearing, she tripped a lot. At that time, no one guessed this somewhat comic attribute was a forecast of something much darker down the road.

When this scholar graduated from high school and headed to college, her teachers and friends most often described Becky as a world-changer. She was the kind of kid who saw beyond the moment and into the future. That remarkable vision that caused her to note and react to the world around her would no doubt pave the way for great things.

Becky took Utah State by storm. Like a force of nature, she moved from class to class. People might have been initially attracted by her charm and vitality, but they also coveted her friendship because she cared enough to get to know them. She was a listener and friend to many, a young woman who seemed to bring others insight and hope.

It was during her freshman year Becky met a dynamic, charismatic, handsome boy. A simple friendship turned into love, and the Utah State coed was sure that she and Steve Andrews would soon live a fairytale life. But even the sunshine created by the success of her first year in college and the promise of everlasting love couldn't push all the clouds out of her world. There were problems now visiting that went beyond tripping over a stair every now and then. But what finally pushed Becky into seeking a medical evaluation had nothing to do with her vision; she was experiencing tingling in her hands.

A general practitioner examined Becky and suggested she make an appointment with a neurologist. When a seemingly minor problem turned into a visit with a brain specialist, even the eighteen-year-old's optimistic attitude and faith were challenged. What did it mean? Perhaps what she was dealing with was a tumor. Maybe, just as it seemed her life was about to really take off, she was looking at her last days. She never before considered her own mortality, and as she waited for her appointment, the fragility of life was put into very sharp focus. How long would it take and how many tests would she have to endure to be given a medical verdict?

The nature of her problem would not be uncovered by an MRI or CT scan but by something far more simple. The neurologist asked Becky to put her hands out in front of her face at eye level. He then instructed her to slowly move her hands to the sides and to stop when she could no longer see her fingers. When her hands quickly disappeared from her view, the doctor nodded, grimly smiled, and suggested she see an ophthalmologist.

On the surface, the news seemed good. Things were fine inside her head, and that made every other issue appear routine. Becky figured after a few more tests, she'd be given a prescription for corrective glasses and life would once again be back to normal. As it turned out, the news she received would shake her family to the core.

The ophthalmologist quickly uncovered not just the reason for Becky's current medical issues but also the cause of her clumsiness. She had been losing peripheral vision for years. The change had been so gradual that she had not noticed that her range of vision was growing narrower with each new day. Worse yet, there was no turning back the clock through medical science. All the tests proved the young woman had retinitis pigmentosa, which in time would leave her completely blind. The physician estimated that she would lose her sight by the time she was thirty.

Becky heard the diagnosis and fully understood it, but she didn't accept it. Hence, when she left the office, the last thing on her mind was preparing for a sightless future. Her only acknowledgment that she might go blind was when she gave Steve a chance to back out of their engagement. Though he likely more fully grasped her situation than she did, it did not change or affect his love. He was fully committed to her both in sickness and in health.

Within a year, as her vision continued to fade, they were married. The couple started a family, she graduated with a degree in business, and a few years later they moved to Salt Lake City. While the focus of her life was now centered on her children, Natalie and Kendall, Becky also was working part-time. For the

Georgie the yellow Lab helps Becky Andrews not only with her day-to-day tasks but also in her work as a counselor.

moment she could pretend that everything was normal and that nothing would ever change. Yet for this mother, fantasy couldn't build a bridge to reality. By her late twenties, she could no longer ignore the diagnosis she'd been given as a college freshman. Though she wouldn't admit it to friends, even Becky privately acknowledged she was rapidly going blind.

In the early '90s, just after turning in her restricted driver's license, her diminished vision hit her in the face when she walked into a stop sign. Embarrassed and bleeding, she realized changes were coming. She also began using a cane to find objects she could no longer see. As her vision grew darker, so did her mood. Becky was now frustrated not only by what she could no longer see but also by the limits her emerging disability was placing on her life. She couldn't take her kids to school or go shopping, she wasn't really seeing their school presentations, and it took her more than an hour to get to work using city transportation. For the first time in her life, she was scared.

There are essentially two kinds of darkness. The first is created by a world void of light. The second is the darkness brought on by limitations. In the first, you can still dream; but in the second, your dreams are chained by harsh reality. That "I can't do that" thinking brings sadness and depression.

The clouds rapidly gathering in Becky's world brought with them an unexpected fear. By 1997, her lack of vision caused her to hesitate when she walked down a street or rode a bus. Becky's world was shrinking, and her limitations were being magnified. The once-determined independent woman was now feeling trapped. Being alone in an unfamiliar area was often terrifying. If she were scared to move freely, if she needed help at every turn, then what kind of future would be open to her? She didn't want to be a burden on others or spend the rest of her life homebound.

Just as he hadn't given up on Becky when she learned she was going to someday go blind, Steve wasn't going to give up on her now. He still saw his wife as beautiful and bright, and he fully believed in her gifts and potential and recognized that the world still needed her talents. So while there was nothing he could do about the void of light caused by her blindness, he could knock down the limits that Becky and others perceived had been created by her loss of sight. Thus, he began looking for tactics to get her back into the world. He figured the best way to give her a push was to provide her with a companion. So with cheerleader-like enthusiasm, he suggested Becky get a guide dog. Ironically, what should have offered a ray of hope actually brought out old fears. As a child, Becky had been bitten by a dog and thus was terrified of them. So how could she learn to trust something with her safety if she were deeply frightened each time it was in her presence? It would take the encouragement of her family before she began to waver. Finally, wanting to escape a severely limited world and be with her children as their lives expanded trumped her apprehension. Putting childhood fears behind her, she made a giant leap of faith.

The organization Becky turned to was Guide Dogs for the Blind. After applications were completed, representatives of this well-respected organization met with Becky and her family. The meeting assessed the woman's needs, goals, and environment. Because of her positive attitude, her outstanding physical condition, and the support of her family, she was deemed a perfect candidate for the program. Yet, as she would quickly find out, just passing the accepted criteria was only a small part of the process. Now the mother and wife would have to spend a month away from home, living in a dorm, being surrounded by strangers, and learning a new way to view life (the training is now only two weeks). For someone who was so close to her family and whose home had become a security blanket, the sacrifice seemed overwhelming. But it was that same family she feared she was deserting that wanted her to regain her independence. In a sense, they became what she had once been: someone who lifted others up during the hard times. With the approval and encouragement of those around her, on September 17, 1997, she boarded a plane for Oregon. Though doubts still persisted, Becky would later mark this as the day she took her first steps out of the darkness.

Boring, Oregon, is thirty minutes outside Portland. Named for an early settler, William H. Boring, the community of eight thousand was founded as a railroad town but is now known as a vital part of America's lumber industry. Located at the far northern edge of the state, it is a much different place than Salt Lake.

When Becky arrived at Guide Dog's campus, it was still shiny and new. Though the organization dated back to the days just after World War II, the Oregon school didn't open until 1995. Thus, to the local citizens, seeing guide dogs leading students around the community was still a novelty. Yet, with its welcoming attitude and varied landscape, the wooded area seemed a perfect place to build a working relationship between unsure humans and well-trained dogs.

From the night she arrived, Becky was homesick for her family. She missed the noise and the routine that came from having two middle school kids and their friends parading in and out of her home. She also longed for the afternoon walks and late-evening talks with her husband. But now, with the security blanket that was her normal-if-limited life ripped away, she was immersed in a strange world filled with new voices and sounds. And everywhere she turned was a relative of the animal that had bitten her as a child. This experience was going to challenge Becky's grit, determination, and will. She felt so alone, but sixty pounds of tail-wagging fur was about to change her attitude and future in ways that no one could have predicted.

As she met other students, as she listened to her instructors, and as she came to know the excited but focused dogs that had been specially matched to each student, Becky began to adopt a new attitude. She told herself, You first find a way, and then you find your way, and you will make it because there is a buddy at your side.

For the last few years, because she was afraid of running into things, Becky had almost crept through life. Her pace was slow and her steps unsure. But now a yellow Labrador named Pantera was bent on changing her gears. The outgoing "driven to perform dog" demanded to be trusted. She saw no reason to allow Becky to feel her way along a walk or through a room. In her mind, time was wasting and they needed to pick up the pace. At first, she literally pulled the young woman into the unknown, and it was overwhelming. But as Becky learned to trust Pantera, her fears faded, her confidence grew, and moving without fear was exhilarating! She hadn't felt this kind of rush in years. And being able to walk at a rapid pace was just the beginning. As the weeks passed and the training intensified, the two were turned loose in the community. Becky rediscovered the "I can do anything" attitude that had propelled her through high school and college. In a sense, she wasn't blind anymore. She had eyes she trusted, and that trust meant everything.

When her husband, children, parents, grandma, and brother traveled to Boring to attend her graduation, they were shocked by the woman they met. Becky was graceful, self-reliant, and fearless. Steve was seeing the woman he'd met in college, and the kids were being introduced to a person they had never known. They were viewing their mother in a new light, and they sensed she was seeing them in a new way as well. And the dog, with her bright eyes and gaping smile, was simply beyond cool.

As Becky and Pantera showed Steve, Natalie, and Kendall around campus, they were constantly calling out, "Mom, slow down, we can't keep up." The woman, who a month before had been scared of the unknown and often took steps with great hesitation, was now fearlessly rushing ahead. As she marched forward, she was no longer talking about the limits created by her disability; she was rapidly sharing her new ambitions and dreams. Just as she had in high school, she saw a bright future ahead and was going to embrace it with every ounce of her being. She wanted to go hit the mall, go hiking, explore new areas of town, and even go back to school. She couldn't wait to pack her bags, get on the plane, and let Salt Lake meet the woman she'd rediscovered in Oregon.

As she and Pantera settled into their routine in Salt

Lake and returned to work at the Moran Eye Center, Becky wanted to see more of the world. No longer was blindness a roadblock; it was just an obstacle.

With no fears or hesitation, Becky went back to college to earn a master's degree in psychology counseling. Pantera was with her every step of the way. In her spare time, she began to run with Steve by employing a tether. When Steve wasn't around, Pantera was there to train with Becky. In fact, it was the dog who nudged her so much and so hard that Becky decided to celebrate her fortieth birthday by competing in a half marathon. She ran 13.1 miles with Steve as her guide and Pantera waiting at the finish line to greet her. This was more than just an accomplishment; it was a reflection of Becky's new belief in herself and her potential. She couldn't be stopped.

She took a job with Lifeline Adolescent Treatment Center as a therapist for troubled youth. Many of those she counseled had been convicted of crimes and were angry, unpredictable, and antisocial. They likely initially viewed the small, thin, blind woman with disdain and contempt. Just a few years before, when Becky was almost scared to leave her home, just being in the same room with these young men would have shaken her to the core. But having Pantera—who always put Becky's life ahead of his own—by her side gave her the confidence to do her job and tear down the walls built by years of mistrust and pain. For a few sessions, Pantera was a bodyguard, yet the dog's role quickly grew by providing the kids with something to talk about. The canine bridged a gap that opened up trust between the therapist and her clients. Thus, not only was Pantera pushing Becky's potential but her new job was also expanding the dog's role. He was now a partner in her work too.

Pantera also quickly fell into the role of a childcare specialist. When the family was on outings, the Lab's range of vision carried well beyond just Becky. He kept Natalie and Kendall in sight too. Becky fully recognized this on August 11, 1999, when she took Kendall shopping for school supplies at a downtown Salt Lake City mall. After hitting several stores and purchasing most of what they needed, Becky found herself short on cash. Even though Kendall was old enough to be left on his own and the dog had never had a problem doing this in normal circumstances, today, when Becky tried to walk outside of the store, Pantera did not want to leave. After Becky ordered Pantera forward, the dog led her out of the mall, across the street, and to an ATM machine. As they walked back to the door to cross the street, there was a stillness; the street was quiet, and no one was outside. While

Becky wondered why it was so quiet, Pantera seemed driven to get back to Kendall. The woman would later learn that a tornado had just touched down close by. Her comforting words did nothing to calm him down. Before she could stuff her money into her purse, Pantera urgently began pulling her back across the street. Unable to get him to slow down, a confused Becky fell into step. As soon as they entered the mall, the dog calmly guided Becky to Kendall. Once they were reunited, Pantera urged them to move farther into the store. A few seconds later, the power went out and they were plunged into darkness as a tornado ripped down the same street the dog and woman had just crossed. The unexpected twister would cause $150 million in damage, kill one person, and injure more than 150 others. Judging by the damage outside the mall, there would have been one more death if Pantera hadn't literally run Becky across the street and back into the building.

It was then an epiphany struck. This dog was not just a vehicle that opened up the world to a blind woman; it was an intelligent creature who could somehow sense dangers and steer people out of harm's way. So he was a life builder and lifesaver.

Though he never again saved her from a tornado, for several more years, Pantera was a full partner to

Becky the wife, mother, and therapist. Leading her each step of the way, Pantera grew as Becky grew, and his role at home and at work expanded, as did Becky's. Pantera allowed her once more to embrace the optimistic and empathetic nature that was such a vital part of her youth. Because of her canine guide, she was able to direct hundreds of suffering souls through the greatest storms in their lives and steer them back to a road filled with hope.

After several years as a therapist with different agencies, Becky started her own business. Pantera was there for the ribbon cutting before retiring and being replaced by Cricket. A now fully confident Becky no longer needed a dog to provide her with courage; so the role Cricket played in her life was different than that of her first guide dog. At Resilient Solutions, an individual, marriage, and family therapy practice employing fifteen human therapists and one Labrador that might well be just as valuable, clients poured out their emotions as they dealt with loss. As if able to sense clients' pain, when they no longer could talk, Cricket would get up, walk across the room, and give the clients a chance to pet her. This simple act seemed to put things into perspective and to reopen the lines of communication and healing. Just like Pantera was not trained to avoid a tornado, Cricket was not instructed in how to help humans deal with grief. She just grew into that role. After Cricket was retired, another guide dog, Georgie, stepped into the same role. She also shares her calming and healing spirit with Becky's clients.

In 2013, Becky was honored in New York City as the National Mother of Achievement. Accepting the award with the nationally known therapist was her partner, a yellow companion that seemed to be constantly looking for new worlds to explore. From a girl who once feared dogs to a woman who now fully trusted dogs as her eyes and partners in work and life, Becky Andrews continues to naturally share her gifts of comfort, encouragement, and compassion with those who have lost all hope. As her dogs have guided her out of a very dark place, she guides others into a world without fear.

Ignoring Barriers

A barrier is of ideas, not of things.

Mark Caine

There is something born into a few individuals that drives them to reach beyond normal human boundaries. They dream of things that supposedly can't be done and do things that others do not dream of. But their greatest achievements are usually not accomplished alone. In the end, they find it is teamwork that allows them to do things that few have ever imagined.

Trevor Thomas was born to move. It seemed to be in his DNA. By the time he began to walk through his parents' home in Elkhart, Indiana, everyone had problems keeping up with him. He was downhill skiing by the age of three and already racing bikes down steep hills when he entered elementary school. As he grew into his teens, he tried every sport he could find, challenged every ride at amusement parks, and even dreamed of climbing mountains. By the time he was enrolled at the University of Colorado, normal sports no longer gave him the thrills he craved, so he threw himself into extreme activities such as skydiving, backcountry skiing, and racing cars. Those around Trevor thought of him as a strong, independent visionary who, if born a few hundred years earlier, would have been exploring the new world with Lewis and Clark or sailing the seven seas with Magellan.

After earning his college degree, he became an event planner. Using the creative part of his nature, he set up everything from small conferences to large conventions. Building on his success, he moved into asset recovery and, later, corporate sales. Still, at the heart of everything he did was the lure of seeking out new ways to challenge his agility, reactions, and courage. He felt he was most alive when living on the edge. Thus, his work was merely a means to pave the way back to his passion of facing new tests and encountering new obstacles.

He was in his thirties when he opted to take a break from the real world and go back to school in

Nevada. His years in business had given him an up-close and personal look at the legal machine in motion, thus providing a thirst to learn more about law. But for a man who relished each moment spent in the great outdoors, there was a big price to pay. He was now forced to all but live in classrooms and libraries, reading as much as fourteen hours a day. While challenging his mind like he once had his body, he noticed a slight change in his vision.

As the hobbies that drove his life depended upon perfect vision, the last thing the adventurer wanted was to wear glasses. Initially he figured if he gave himself a break from reading, his sight would return to normal. It didn't. Soon he was straining as he walked up a street or drove his car. Worse yet, the colors he'd relished when exploring nature were turning into shades of gray and black.

More perturbed than worried, Trevor made an appointment with an optometrist. He was then sent to a vision specialist and then to a regular doctor. It took several tests before he was diagnosed with a possible autoimmune disorder. His body saw his eyes as invaders and was doing everything it could to shut them down. The worst news was that nothing could be done. All the experts agreed that Trevor would be completely blind within months.

Some greet news like this with denial and others
with sad acceptance; Trevor reacted with anger. How
could this happen to him? He had challenged mountain trails, roaring rapids, and uncharted ski slopes.
His dreams centered on physically pushing his body
and his courage to the limits. He defined himself by
the risks he took and the adventures he experienced.
Without that thrill and rush, life was simply not
appealing.

As his vision quickly faded, so did Trevor's will to
live. With the blindness came things he'd never before experienced or even acknowledged: stress and a
complete lack of confidence. For a man whose life had
once had no limits, the new reality was claustrophobic.
It was as if he was trapped in a dark room, the walls
were closing in, and he could do nothing except wait
for the last bit of light to fade from his life and extin-
guish all hope.

Now Trevor's dreams of seeking out the passion in
life had become nightmares of being surrounded by
boredom. He saw himself with little value and almost
no future. What could he do to keep from being a burden to his family and friends?

Charlotte, North Carolina, was not an easy community to navigate for those with perfect vision; but for a
newly blind person, it was a nightmare. Trevor used to

dash from one store to another, but without his sight, nothing seemed the same and every step was made in fear. With no visual landmarks, just navigating a block seemed like a bigger challenge than skiing down a steep mountain. On top of that, the noises were louder—at times almost deafening—and odors were much more intense too. With fear and frustration his constant companions, he seemed to have lost all control of even the simplest areas of his life.

Trevor realized he was going to have to gain new skills in order to have any hope of living on his own. The first task was learning how to use a cane. Employing this special tool for the blind got him outside his door, but it didn't do much to open up his world. He was forced to move slowly and was constantly depending upon others for directions and information. With each new day it became more evident that he was no longer the master of his world. Even the act of purchasing groceries or coffee emphasized his dependence. Although a blind person can distinguish a quarter from a nickel, there is no real difference in paper money. Thus, Trevor had to trust others not to take advantage of him.

His friends would not give up on Trevor. They kept dragging him out of his dark world by finding ways to include him in their experiences. As he felt more like a passenger or fifth wheel, their efforts brought the man little encouragement. When a friend offered to take him to hear Erik Weihenmayer speak, the bottom really dropped out. It seemed like a slap in the face.

Weihenmayer had gone blind as a child but decided he was not going to let sightlessness stop him from being completely involved in the world. Taking on any new challenge that he was given, he found a way to try almost all the regular activities of youth. In high school, he became a champion wrestler and discovered he had a knack for rock climbing. In both of those seemingly different sports, he found his touch was so sensitive he could feel holds that others couldn't see. After completing college and landing a teaching position, he used summers to hone his climbing talents. He'd come to Charlotte to talk about meeting his ultimate goal of doing something no blind person had ever accomplished: scaling Mount Everest.

The last thing Trevor wanted was to hear a blind person speak. He already knew the challenges of daily life, so why would he want to listen to another blind person talk about living in a dark world? Yet because his friend wouldn't stop nagging him, Trevor grudgingly agreed to attend the event. Surprisingly it was an illuminating moment. The words he heard that night provided the blind man with a new vision.

Trevor Thomas with Tennille, who adapted wonderfully
to the lifestyle of a hiker.

"A spark of greatness exists in all people, but only by touching that spark to adversity's flame does it blaze into the force that fuels our lives and the world."

Weihenmayer's words were not just something to think about; they were a challenge. If this man could climb the seven highest peaks in the world, then there was hope. As feeling sorry for what Trevor had lost served no purpose, it was time to inventory what he had left and build a few new dreams.

After the program, the two men met. As they exchanged stories of their lives and challenges, Weihenmayer gave Trevor a verbal seed that took root. From time to time it's OK to be foolish. After all, it was foolish for a blind man to challenge Mount Everest. Everyone told him it couldn't be done, and yet Weihenmayer found a way to do it. In the process, he inspired thousands to try something that others told them they'd never be able to do. So what foolish thing could Trevor attempt that would help him regain his value and self-worth?

Trevor had recently gone on hikes through the local woods with a friend. Though doing anything at a slow pace was against his nature, and he stumbled time and time again, he found an unexpected joy in being away from the city and hearing the music of a new world. When he'd rushed down mountains on skis or bikes, when he'd raced cars, he had been in too much of a hurry to note a bird's song or the gentle rustling of leaves in the wind. Yet when he was walking along a trail, he heard all that and more. A small lizard racing along a rock drew his attention, as did the almost silent footsteps of a squirrel climbing a tree. To go along with the "music" of nature were smells that brought visions of beauty he had never before noticed. The more he walked and the deeper into the woods he traveled, the more his senses burst to life. He soon discovered that by listening to his own voice, he could sense how far he was from a tree or a cliff face.

In 2008, Weihenmayer's challenge to living a bit

foolishly and defy others' limited expectations propelled Trevor to seize a new goal and dream a new dream. He was going to become the first blind person to hike the entire length of the Appalachian Trail solo. At first his friends and family cautioned against attempting something that "foolish." After all, a lot of sighted people had died trying to hike this challenging trail. But thanks to his new confidence, they began to believe in him. As he bought the equipment needed for the task, a local outfitter helped him choose the best equipment for his needs.

Trevor had no goals beyond completing his mission. He wasn't looking at this as a career opportunity; he simply saw the trek as a chance to reclaim his independence. If he were able to finish the more than two thousand miles, he would no longer be just blind Trevor Thomas; he would be a man who once again had value.

The Appalachian Trail experience was more difficult than he could have imagined. He fought off cold, heat, rain, and snow. He slipped and fell and had to pull himself up more times than he could count. Isolation spread like a haunting fog magnifying his fears. He had encounters with bears, coyotes, raccoons, snakes, and insects. He marched through illness and hunger. Day after day there was the fear of making a wrong turn. And even though he grew tired of sleeping in the damp, cold woods and the injuries that accompanied his many falls, he never gave up. Six months after taking his first step on the impossible mission, he proved everyone wrong and finished. As others celebrated his accomplishment, the question asked most was, "What are you going to do next?" Most hoped Trevor would opt to find a real job and a new hobby. Instead he embraced another round of "foolishness" and signed onto the challenge of trekking the Pacific Crest Trail. This trail, because of its varying climate and terrain, was even more challenging than the Appalachian Trail. When he finished at the Canadian border with team members he had convinced to go with him, he realized he had found his real passion. The dangers and challenges he faced had helped him restoke his thirst for living.

Thanks to the publicity of being the first blind person to conquer America's two most famous hiking trails, in the small world of extreme hikers, he was famous. A host of different companies sought his endorsements for their equipment. Yet to continue to grow his new income source, he was going to have to face even more difficult challenges. After navigating swamps and deserts to get his juices flowing, in 2011, Trevor flew west to take on the Colorado Trail.

For the uninformed, the Colorado Trail may seem

like a cakewalk when compared to the 2,100 miles
a person has to cover to complete the Appalachian
Trail or the 2,600 miles, starting in Mexico and end-
ing in Canada, that make up the Pacific Crest Trail.
After all, the Colorado Trail is just 489 miles long. It
begins in Denver and ends in Durango. Yet because of
the steep cliffs, grueling grades, deep snowfields, and
bears and mountain lions, few sighted people take on
this extreme challenge. Not only does it offer a doz-
en different ways to die but also the path is not well
defined, and it is easy to miss the trail markers. One
wrong turn makes it almost impossible to find your
way back. In other words, it was the trail of Trevor's
dreams.

Trevor flew to Denver to meet up with an experienced, sighted hiker who was going to be his guide.
When the man didn't show, Trevor decided to make
the trek on his own. It didn't take long for him to
discover he'd bitten off more than he could chew.
Facing failure for the first time in his hiking career,
he returned home wondering if he had hit a wall that
couldn't be climbed.

Over the course of several years of walking along
trails, Trevor had honed almost bat-like skills. He
could actually tell distances and sense grades with his
voice and ears. But those skills did no good at noting

obstacles in his path, such as downed trees and rock slides, and they couldn't alert him to predatory animals. So the extreme trails—the ones he really wanted to challenge—could not be managed without eyes.

Once back home, Trevor began to analyze how he could continue to maintain his independence while meeting the punishing challenges brought on by the likes of the Colorado Trail. It seemed that adding a permanent human member to his team was the only answer. Yet by doing that, wasn't he admitting his blindness was a limiting factor in pursuing his dreams? And, as there were now so many people with sight limitations looking to him as their hero, wouldn't acknowledging that he was not able to pursue his dreams independently cause them to limit their lives as well? Before giving up and giving in by seeking out a human for a partner, Trevor decided to see if a guide dog might work as his hiking companion.

As he was blind but obviously very mobile and motivated to live independently, the task of qualifying and receiving a guide dog seemed easy. But Trevor quickly discovered that most organizations were not interested in matching him with a trained dog. It seemed as though guide dogs were for blind people who lived in urban areas. He was told time and time again that a dog simply couldn't learn the skills needed to attempt dangerous treks through the wilderness. Only one organization, Guide Dogs for the Blind, gave him a chance to explain his vision. After evaluating his goals and needs, the school began the task of finding a dog that was athletic enough to keep up with the country's most famous blind hiker. It would be an agile black Lab that best fit the qualifications.

Tennille was athletic, strong, energetic, and smart. But she also was blessed with another trait that made her the perfect match for Trevor; she was an instinctive problem solver. After a trip west and two weeks of bonding and instruction on the Guide Dogs for the Blind campus, the man and dog became a team. During that time, his trainer, Larissa, realized that it would be impossible to teach Trevor everything he would need to know regarding backcountry navigation. So she taught him how Tennille learned so that he could continue to work with her. With the initial training finished, the pair flew to North Carolina where the real work began.

For the first few weeks, Trevor and Tennille met the challenges of Charlotte. Within days the man discovered the dog had put him in the fast lane. Unlike with his cane, with the dog as his guide, he was getting from place to place almost effortlessly. But he wondered how this would translate to the woods.

Tennille understood curbs, stop signs, and cars. She could warn Trevor about all the obstacles found in city life. But the trails were a different matter. She was going to have see signs and take him to them. She was going to have to warn him of low tree branches and dangerous ice. She had to recognize rock slides and guide the man away from a thousand-foot drop-off while traversing a trail only eighteen inches wide. She was also going to have to recognize dangerous predators both large and small. To train her to face elements found only in the isolated wilderness, Trevor had to expose the dog to all kind of different situations in the controlled environments he knew. Would she be able to assimilate all the different and varying dangers of nature in order to allow him to pursue his dreams of taking on the country's most challenging trails without another human? It didn't take the dog long to pass every test Trevor created. Now it was time for the dog to teach the man.

Trevor had exceeded all the expectations for a blind person because of his thirst for independence, but Tennille was not a tool; she was a team member. He was going to have to trust her as much as she trusted him. When she stopped, he was going to have to value her judgment that something was wrong rather than just order her forward. He found this out the hard way in a swamp. When Tennille stopped, Trevor pushed on, and Tennille refused; he soon realized she was right. If he had moved forward, he would have stepped on a rattlesnake. That made a deep impression. From then on, if the Lab stopped, he would trust her judgment and stop too.

As the two became a team, and as they spent more time alone in the woods, Trevor began to talk to Tennille as if she were another person. He would explain almost everything they found along the trails. Within a few months and several hundred miles of walking, he discovered the dog's vocabulary was growing. By the time the man felt secure enough to challenge the Colorado Trail, the dog knew and understood more than 500 words.

Walking any trail is a matter of connecting the dots. You have to go from one marker or landmark to another. In places like Colorado, the extreme weather changes and the storms that come with them—felled trees, mud, and rock slides—could change the course of creeks and make the markers more difficult to find. Even when you can see the landscape, it is all but impossible to figure out which direction to go. But if you can't see and you come across a rock slide and have to make a detour, the challenge is magnified. One wrong turn and you are completely lost. For a hiker with only the food he can carry on his back, the survival clock ticks quickly as he frantically tries to find a landmark pointing him in the right direction. This is what makes extreme hiking so dangerous and why it also provides such a rush. The deeper into the wilderness you go, the more you live on the edge between life and death.

Tennille proved to be a better partner than most humans. She sensed danger well before a man could. In fact, the dog's presence likely drove off most of the curious predators before the man could even sense their presence on the challenging Colorado Trail. She also easily found the trail signs and rock cairns, navigated around rock slides, and warned him of all tree limbs that could have knocked him off his feet. She had no problems finding the right place to cross creeks or banks of snow. She even told him when it was time to rest. Not that she ever got tired; she just made sure he took his breaks. As they sat together on top of mountain peaks, he got the idea she was marveling at the sights he could not see. With each new day and adventure, the dog was as thrilled as he was to be hitting the trail. Most important, they did what most thought was impossible by completing one of the nation's most dangerous treks.

Trevor has hiked more than 20,000 miles in his career, but none have been more rewarding than the past three and a half years the pair has hiked together, completing 6,000 miles and five thru hikes and summiting countless mountains, including Colorado's tallest peak. Trevor has learned to completely trust Tennille's perceptions and judgment. She knows the dangers he can't see and protects him from 1,000-foot drops, bears, and cars.

This marriage of man and dog and the incredible adventures they have lived have inspired thousands of disabled people to push society in recognizing that limits should not be placed on those with disabilities. Because of his amazing accomplishments, Trevor has become a media star. Through television, social media, and print stories, he has also become a hero to thousands. He founded Team FarSight Foundation to give blind kids a chance to gain independence and value through wilderness experiences. Yet his teaming with the black Lab has done something else, too. It has stretched the boundaries society once applied to guide dogs. In an extreme fashion Trevor has proved that a well-trained canine is constantly growing and expanding its role. As Tennille has shown, there are no limits to where guide dogs can go or what they can learn. And with a guide dog leading the way, Trevor goes to places few have been, and, in his own way, sees things only a handful of people have ever seen.

Unconditional

The greatest gift that you can give to others is the gift of unconditional love and acceptance.

Brian Tracy

Love ignites fires that provide light in the darkest places on earth. That love has the power to create miracles if it is accompanied by just a bit of faith. And when the love is strong enough, even those of whom little is expected can touch the world in ways few can fathom.

The special love between a father and a son creates a bond unlike any other. It has been written about in books, movies, and plays. In the early 1960s, Paul Petersen even scored a hit record with the song "My Dad." The lyrics in that song spoke volumes about

what it meant to have a father who was not just a role
model but also the person who most deeply believed
in your potential. One line is, "When I was small, I felt
ten foot tall when I was by his side." There are many
men who have invested so much faith in their children they deserve that kind of honor, and one of these
fathers is Phil Stevens.

On a very special day, Phil welcomed three boys
into his home. Two of the triplets were healthy, but the
other—a boy whom the Stevenses named Jared—was
born with cerebral palsy, a condition that could have
severely limited his life. In this case, this dad was not
going to let that happen.

Cerebral palsy strikes two in every 1,000 children.
There are various levels of the disease. In its most
severe form, the cruel intruder robs its host of muscle
and voice control and mental development. Because
of the awkwardness in movement and speech, they
are often avoided. It can be a very lonely world where
isolation is the norm, even when surrounded by a
crowd.

As he grew, Jared faced a number of physical roadblocks that inhibited his interaction with the world.
His speech was also affected, making communication
often difficult and frustrating. But mentally he was
as sharp as a tack. His father wanted others to see the

bright child with the quick wit, not the boy who had a body that functioned at the level of a sixth-month-old child. But how do you get people to look beyond a boy using a wheelchair? How do you get people to understand that inside that body is a brain that is actually functioning far above age level? How could he penetrate the walls and get others to realize that the thin young man with the bright eyes and crooked smile was a creative, dynamic force struggling to be recognized?

The first step in giving his son a full life was allowing him to be a part of the world. The Stevenses were not going to allow their son to miss out on the adventures his brothers were enjoying every day. So Jared, usually with his father, Phil, pushing him, was taken to ball games, restaurants, and on vacations, no matter how challenging. He was a part of sports teams and even became a Boy Scout. Although Jared was treated like everyone else wherever possible, there were limits to what his parents could accomplish. Those limits were not as much created by Jared's physical limitations as by society's views of those who are physically disabled, which were evident when the family was out in public.

Pushing Jared down the street created a parting of human seas. The wheelchair was so intimidating, many circled as far around it as possible. Children

Jared's age had little patience with a boy who physically couldn't keep up with them. Then there was
the matter of language. Because of cerebral palsy's
effect on his throat, chest, and vocal chords, learning
to understand Jared required time. Few were patient
enough to give the boy a chance to share his thoughts
and ideas. And because he didn't have the chance to
finish his thoughts, most didn't realize how bright
he was.

Jared moved through elementary school effortlessly, learning everything he was given. Though his
teachers had to adapt to meet his special needs, he
mastered his coursework with ease. Yet making close
friends was far more difficult. He was perceived as the
kid with a disability before he was thought of as Jared.
Sadly, there seemed no way to open up minds and get
his peers to see past the dramatic effects that cerebral
palsy had inflicted on his body.

At home it was easier. To his family, his wit, charm,
and intelligence were recognized, and he was easily
understood. Though it surprised many visitors, Jared
loved the things every other middle school kid enjoyed. Even with limited movement and dexterity, he
was a whiz at video games. His sharp mind gave him
an edge in anticipating what reaction would be needed
next, and that meant he was usually one step ahead of

the game. Yet when he dropped a controller, he had no way of retrieving it. Thus, it fell upon those around him to do that simple task. Jared also couldn't take off his own socks or pick up the television remote, and he needed help opening doors. Yet what he required more than any of those things was to be appreciated and accepted rather than pitied and shunned.

Good parents never give up on their children. No matter how high the hurdle, they search for ways to climb over it. The Stevenses were not going to allow their son to be homebound. His mind was good, he had a great personality and sharp wit, and they were going to find a method to expose all that was special in Jared to the world.

Phil happened upon a story about a service dog that enabled a paralyzed person to accomplish the basic tasks of his life. The dog opened the man's doors, picked up clothing, handed him the mail, and even pulled his wheelchair. As he considered his son's daily needs, Phil sensed a dog might be a way for Jared to gain a bit of independence and freedom. A call to Canine Companions for Independence opened a new door for this boy who used a wheelchair.

The organization studied the Stevenses' Nashville, Tennessee, home and got to know Jared as a person. Representatives from Canine Companions looked into the boy's limitations while also studying his strengths. They determined Jared was a very good candidate for a service dog. The question was now in the family's court: Would they be willing to go to the organization's Southeast Region Training Center in Orlando and spend a few weeks learning how to properly use and take care of a dog? Without hesitation they answered in the affirmative, all the while praying that 2012 would be the year that Jared's life would dramatically change.

It takes more than two years of training to get an assistance dog ready to serve a person with a disability. During this time, the dog is taught scores of commands that require prompt actions. It is relatively easy to get a dog to perform those learned skills in a controlled environment, but a great deal of an assistance dog's work comes in a world filled with noise and distractions. Only by continuing to correctly perform their duties in ballparks, malls, schools, and on busy streets does the dog earn the chance to serve.

Just like that of any junior-high-aged boy, Jared's life was in constant change. Because of his parents' push to keep him active in the world, he was involved in everything from church to Boy Scouts. Therefore, his assistance dog would be out in the public a great deal. There would also be the noise of TV, video games, and music that go along with a child in the information age. On top of that, cerebral palsy had affected Jared's voice and speech patterns, so when he asked for something, the dog was going to have to learn to recognize the commands. This would require a very special animal with an adaptive skill set.

During training the Stevenses met a cream-colored Labrador/golden retriever cross named John III. The twinkle in Jared's eyes and the dog's vigorously wagging tail told the Stevenses there was hope. Yet it would be several months before they realized this was more than just an immediate bond between a boy and a dog. This was the forming of a team that would soon unlock a very stubborn door.

John III learned and adapted quickly to Jared's voice, but even more remarkably, he just as rapidly seemed to be able to read Jared's body language. Even before they graduated from training, the dog was studying the boy's facial expressions as a way of gauging if he was setting something to the side or if he had dropped it and needed John III to pick it up and give it back to him. But the real benefit of what John III was bringing to the table would only be fully realized when the pair came home.

Back in Tennessee, John III quickly got to know his new home, including Jared's siblings, and figured out his place in this new world. On command, John III could do the chores that Jared would otherwise need help from his family members to accomplish. John retrieved clothing, pencils, and toys and delivered them to Jared. Yet what was most remarkable was the way the dog looked at the boy. There was love and acceptance in that gaze, and Jared picked up on it. Jared knew that John III did not see his disability. So while John III was there to deal with Jared's practical needs, within days he had begun to benefit him emotionally as well. Even in those first weeks, the boy began to refer to the dog as "my best buddy."

A friend sees your strengths and accepts you in spite of your restrictions. Even for those with no physical limitations, friends are not easy to find. But if you struggle with speech and motor skills, it can be difficult to find anyone outside of your family who will open their hearts and arms and surround you with love. John III's tender gift of friendship was the greatest gift the child had ever known.

At home the two "friends" were inseparable. When Jared played video games, John III watched every move, mirroring the boy's frustration when he lost and joy when he won. When the boy read, the dog listened, hanging on every word as if it was a code to unlocking the key to the universe. It is little wonder as the weeks moved forward that the dog's devotion to Jared enhanced the boy's appreciation for himself. It was as if the animal's unconditional love was the formula for transforming the child's sense of value.

No doubt one of the keys to this new point of view was Jared no longer being as dependent upon his parents. John III now did the little things that they used to do for him—from turning on a light or a game console to picking up a book. Thus Jared was gaining a real sense of independence. Making strides toward being a self-reliant person was a huge step in maturity. Without the dog, it was a step that simply couldn't have been taken.

As the boy and dog ventured out into the world, another dramatic transformation occurred. The sea of humanity that had once spread out before and away from Jared and his wheelchair was now coming forward to greet him. People wanted to meet John III. They wanted to pet the dog and find out what he did for the boy. Better yet, people no longer talked "around" Jared; they talked to him. They asked him questions about John III and were so curious they patiently waited for the answers. Although Jared looked different, thanks to John III, people found that the creative Jared had a great deal to share with them. As the boy explained the dog's role, people also began to see the boy's intelligence and insight. These questions led to relationships based not on pity but on commonality. It seemed as if it took a dog for the world to view Jared as a real person.

Jared loved to watch sports on TV but was really drawn to wrestling. When a match was being shown, his eyes were glued to the screen. He rooted for his heroes, and his facial expression fully revealed how they were doing. It didn't take long for John III to get into the matches as well, watching with excitement as he studied the boy's actions and reactions.

When he observed his son watching the sport, Phil sensed another avenue that had the promise of leading the way for his son to interact with kids his own age. He called the coach at Jared's school and asked if the boy could become a part of the wrestling team. He further explained that although cerebral palsy had robbed Jared of his motor skills, he still loved the sport. Even though the experience of actually wrestling was out of the question, if he could just wear a uniform, attend practice, and be a part of the team, it would mean so much to the boy. The coach agreed, and Jared was given the chance to watch practices, listen to instruction, and learn even more about the sport he so loved. He was also placed in the team picture and was able to cheer for his team members when they hit the mat. And at night, as John III lay down by the boy's bed, Jared shared his experiences with the dog as well as his dreams of someday being able to make it out on the mat for a match of his own.

Perhaps it was because the dog attended the meets and watched from the stands as well as the devotion and love of Jared's family, but the coach began seeking a way to make the boy's dream come true. To the shock of every person in the stands, at a home match, the coach picked up Jared from his wheelchair and laid the boy on the mat to represent his school. It was just supposed to be a symbolic act to reward loyalty and show the team's acceptance. But thanks to another young man, it quickly became something much more. The junior high student he was matched against knew that an easy victory was assured. Yet when the referee signaled for the match to begin, this student fell to the ground, grabbed Jared's arm, and pulled the boy over on top of him, setting himself up for the pin. In a matter of just a few seconds, Jared won the match.

People in the stands were both crying and cheering. The celebration continued for several minutes. As Jared's teammates helped him back into his wheelchair, the boy's grin spelled out what had just happened. A video that captured that match was posted on YouTube and went viral. Within weeks it had been shared and viewed by millions. *Good Morning America* even invited Jared to New York to be a guest on the ABC morning show. The boy's answer was a qualified yes. He would be happy to attend if John III accompanied him.

Jared's response fully showed that the boy understood what his dog had brought to his life. John III's view of Jared as a vital, valuable person was the first step in others outside his family understanding his potential, too. The dog had brought people into his life and allowed him to make friends. John III had given him confidence and fueled dreams, one of which had now come true. So as the boy and dog were a team, in Jared's mind, they had to make that trip together to show millions the miracle that had happened thanks to John III.

On *Good Morning America*, the video was shown again. As they introduced Jared and John III, the veteran TV hosts were crying. They told the audience that this was a rare moment when the best of human nature was on display and the potential of the human heart was being honored. During the interview, Olympic wrestler Rulon Gardner—who was perhaps the greatest underdog ever to win a gold medal—marched out onto the set and placed a gold medal around Jared's neck. The American athletic legend then declared that the boy was, in fact, his hero.

Jared's brush with fame did not end with that appearance on network TV. He and John III marched in the 2012 inaugural parade in Washington, DC, and were made a part of the Tennessee Titans football team. On top of that, news outlets all over the world have told about the amazing transformation created in a boy by his service dog. That has led to other people with disabilities obtaining service dogs to enrich their lives.

When a father set in motion getting a dog to help his son with simple tasks around the house, he had no idea he would be unlocking the potential that Jared could offer the world. Jared, now a high school student, is planning on going to college. And thanks to a dog who is able to sense needs and constantly adapt in meeting those needs, the limitations created by Jared's disability are now exceeded by the potential of a mind that has been fully unleashed.

No matter age, race, or position, everyone dreams of being a winner. Winning validates our existence and helps us realize goals. It also brings a sense of acceptance and self-esteem. It was John III who put Jared into a position to be accepted, appreciated, and given a chance to become a winner. It was John III who did the impossible, putting a disorder in its place, as he led a boy into a real world where dreams can and do come true.

Service Forgotten

The nation which forgets its defenders will be itself forgotten.

Calvin Coolidge

Our heroes should not be dismissed or forgotten. They should never be neglected or mistreated. They must be recognized. They need to be honored with thankfulness and respect for their sacrifices. Only by recognizing what they have done for us are we worthy of receiving the gifts they have given through their selfless service.

The smooth-coated collie had been bred and raised in the hopes that he would become a guide dog. Even as a pup he seemed mature beyond his years. While

---

The names of both the woman whom Salty guided and the dog's second owner have been changed to protect their privacy.

others in his litter were playing, he was standing back and studying the scene. His mind seemed to naturally calculate every move and be aware of everything going on around him. Thus, the calm, focused dog reminded his trainer of an old seaman, one who had spent years facing every challenge and in that time had gained great insight and wisdom. As the veterans of sailing were called "Old Salts," the collie was christened Salty.

With his alert gaze and his muscular body, as he grew, Salty stood out from the other dogs around him. He thrived on his trainer's encouragement and was motivated by attention. Even casual observers picked him out as confident, determined, and intelligent. He was also intuitive. He sensed obstacles and problems before they happened. He was therefore a dog who was rarely surprised. When he reached the age of two, Salty was put through a year of intense training. During that time he was pushed through every possible test a guide dog would experience during his lifetime of service. He learned to negotiate busy sidewalks, rural roads, ramps, elevators, large buildings, and metal steps. He was also educated in how to behave while on public transportation and in stores, schools, and restaurants. He was put into situations where there were distractions and temptations. His patience was measured, as was his ability to sense danger and ignore a command in order to keep his handler safe. Daily tasks were repeated, varied, and adapted. As he met these new challenges, his skill set grew and so did his vocabulary. Salty soon recognized and responded to more than fifty commands and was able to sense a dozen more cues delivered by feel through his harness.

The collie had another trait that endeared him to those at the school. He was both loving and loyal. He bonded quickly with those who trained him and always seemed motivated to lay down his life for them. He displayed the courage and convictions of dogs about which stories were written. He was a rare dog who seemed more than ready to embrace the most daunting of tasks.

The US Marines have a slogan: "The few. The proud. The Marines." Those words indicate that, to wear the uniform, a man or woman must be a rare and dedicated individual. Salty carried those same traits. So while others in his class flunked out of guide-dog training, he kept moving forward. If there had been such a ranking in the school, his grades would have made him officer material. In fact, Salty was such a model student that his trainers deemed he was ready to work with any age and in any environment.

Once dogs were certified, the school began to match

human prospects with the newly trained dogs. Just as each canine had a unique aptitude and personality, each one of the men and women who applied had special needs, weaknesses, and strengths. One candidate was an elderly woman from Florida who needed a dog that could recognize and adjust to the physical limitations brought on by her age. Thus, the dog assigned to Emma was going to have to be patient, methodical, and laid-back. Much more than any other dog in his class, Salty matched the woman's very specific and unusual needs.

During their weeks of training at the school, Salty quickly adjusted to Emma. Though she often messed up commands, he learned to understand what she wanted and responded appropriately. He also never hurried, allowing the woman's slow pace to become his own. As the trainers taught Emma how to work the harness, Salty studied her as if memorizing her reactions. He quickly grew to understand her limitations and used his strength to compensate for them. As she patted his head, his eyes sparkled, and it seemed his mouth formed a grin. It was like he knew that Emma was his and he relished the responsibility of meeting her needs. Though it took the woman a while to grasp all the nuances of working in tandem with a dog, with the collie's help, she grew more comfortable with allowing him to do his job. By graduation, she confidently marched across the stage, assured that Salty's eyes were mapping her every step.

The first few days that a blind person and her new guide are at home are often difficult periods of adjustment. The human is not used to having to take care of a dog, and the canine is living in a completely different environment. Yet Salty easily made the adjustment. He learned the features in his new home, found his place in it, and stayed close to Emma as she adapted to meet his needs.

His eyes allowed her to move with so much more ease than she had with her cane. Yet it would be outside the home where he would really transform her life.

For the first time in years, Emma could go out in public without the help of a friend. With the dog leading the way, she now had the opportunity to shop independently, attend church, and ride public transportation. For the first time in years, with Salty leading the way, it felt as though she had no limits or fears.

In a matter of weeks, the canine/human team became a well-known sight around the neighborhood. As people watched the collie lovingly guide the woman, they rushed up to ask questions about how he knew to stop at this point or to warn her about a coming curb or fence. Those who approached Emma always wanted to pet Salty and make him their best friend too. Though he treated each guest with patience and respect, the dog was far too focused on his mistress and her needs to get very close to anyone but her. Hence, he became the woman's shadow. Even when he was off harness, he followed her everywhere she went. He was by her side when she listened to the radio, talked on the phone, or chatted with friends from her porch. Salty was also beside her bed at night, never completely relaxing until he sensed she was asleep. And when she woke up, he bounced forward, ready to again serve her needs.

As the months stretched into years, his focus remained on the woman whom he seemed bred to serve. And because of his incredible work, Salty became a local celebrity. People brought him toys and treats and patted his head. None of the attention went to his head or pulled his gaze from Emma.

For seven years, the collie led Emma. Observers noted that a half a dozen times he kept her from stepping in front of traffic and on countless other occasions prevented her from falling down steps or walking into a sign, tree, or fence. During those moments when tragedy loomed so near, the woman was completely unaware the dog had likely saved her from injury or death. All she really understood was that he brought independence and security into her life.

As Emma aged, her trips out of the house grew less frequent. Other people began to do her shopping and run her errands. The dog who had given her such wonderful independence was now relegated to being more of a companion than a guide. It was a role he accepted with grace and dignity.

Along with Emma's diminishing physical skills, another issue was taking root. Her mind was slipping. Yet even though sometimes the woman forgot to feed him or allowed his water dish to run dry, Salty remained intensely loyal. He remained at her side to make sure her steps were still safe, and when she stumbled, he was there to help her up.

At some point, Emma lost all interest in the dog she had once so treasured. She no longer petted or talked to him. Yet, rather than call the school that had given the collie to her and ask them to find a new home for Salty, the woman gave the dog to a man she barely knew. Her mind and focus were now so far gone that Emma did not even say good-bye to her guide as he was led out the door and to the man's truck. Tom, Salty's new master, took the confused collie out to his rural home, put him in a five-by-five–foot pen, and closed the gate. The dog who had given his life to service now found himself in solitary confinement.

Salty had never spent nights outdoors. He had never been exposed to the elements. He had never been away from human contact. The pen that was now his new home had a dirt floor, a rusty water bowl, and a plastic crate that was too small to offer any shelter. Confused and lonely, Salty began to bark. His new owner screamed from the mobile home's front door for the dog to be quiet. The former guide dog cried out again, and profanity followed. When Salty refused to give up, Tom came out, opened the gate, grabbed the dog by the neck, and beat him. The collie could have not imagined things would quickly grow much worse.

Thanks to the Florida environment, Salty was soon covered with fleas and ticks. His pen was also quickly filled by his own waste. The food he was given was the cheapest the owner could find, and there were no special treats. He was never petted, bathed, or talked to. If Salty asked for attention, he was usually beaten. In the first year he was at the new home, he was likely never taken out of the pen.

He learned to quit barking, but the neighbors reported that the collie cried every time there was a thunderstorm. Unable to get his entire body in the crate, Salty whimpered with each new crack of lightning and roar of thunder. Yet the storms that were scaring him so would ultimately bring some hope.

After watching the dog suffer in a cold rain, a neighbor called the county humane society and reported that a dog was being severely neglected and abused. A few days later, local authorities made a visit to check on Salty. What they found was disturbing. He was standing ankle deep in waste and mud. Not only was the animal filthy, covered with parasites, and dramatically underfed, he was also scared to death. As they approached, the collie kept his head low as if in fear of being beaten. When they opened the pen, they noted a chain collar around Salty's neck that was so rusted it would barely move. It was a wonder the dog had not choked to death.

As horrible as the conditions were, under the law, the authorities could only cite the owner and demand he take better care of the dog. Yet, rather than just walking away, the concerned visitors contacted a local collie rescue group to see if they could get involved. The leader of that organization called Debbie Abbenante who trained both horses and dogs. Fearing the

After a tumultuous few years, Salty found a happy home.

dog would not last much longer, Debbie and a team arranged a visit with Salty's current owner. As expected, the dog's physical condition was appalling, but it was the collie's complete lack of spirit that broke everyone's hearts. They didn't have to guess why Salty tried to hide in the corner of the tiny enclosure. As the team looked through the chain-link, Tom hit the fencing and taunted the dog. He seemed to enjoy making fun of the neglected animal.

After several minutes of discussion, some of it heated, the team convinced Tom to let Debbie take Salty. As she opened the door and tried to coax the shy, frightened, and sick dog from the pen, he shook and moved backward. Debbie sensed Salty was fully expecting to be hit. When she began stroking his dirty, flea-covered head, he leaned a bit closer. Over the next few minutes, as she sat beside him, he began to calm down. Soon, as Tom mocked her from his porch, she was able to lead the collie outside into the yard. After several more calming strokes on his bony back, she put a leash around his neck, and together they walked to the car. The nightmare was over.

Salty's first stop was at the vet. He was checked out, given his shots, and cleaned up. When he arrived at Debbie's, he was introduced to the other dogs as well as to the family's horses and cats. He was also given his first good meal in more than a year. After being bathed and brushed, the collie was allowed to explore his new domain. As Debbie watched the thin, insecure collie walk timidly from room to room, she realized his fragile psyche likely couldn't take another move. So this couldn't be just another rescue where she fostered Salty until a "forever" owner was located. This had to be the final stop. She needed to adopt the ten-year-old dog. Her small farm was where the dog should spend the rest of his life.

As Debbie discovered more about Salty's background, she came to understand how deeply confused the dog had to be. He had been trained never to leave his partner's side, to constantly look for ways to serve her, and to put loyalty above even his own physical needs. Then without warning, he had been thrown into a pen like a piece of garbage. In one night, the bonding and love that he had known since birth were gone and his world had been destroyed. Worst of all, he had served someone well for seven years and there had been no reward, only a hellish existence of pain, isolation, and neglect.

During his first few weeks at the farm, Debbie and her husband smothered Salty with love. In return he was Debbie's constant shadow. Still, for a while, he glanced nervously over his shoulder as if wondering if the man who had treated him so badly would return to take him back to prison. In time those looks stopped; but if someone raised his or her voice, the dog's worried expression proved he had not forgotten the experience.

On a regular basis, Debbie took her ponies and horses to children's birthday parties. The gentle animals would entertain by showing off a wide variety of tricks as well as offering rides. As he settled into life on the farm, Salty accompanied the woman to these parties. The children loved the friendly collie as much as they did the horses. As he attended more and more of the outings, the shyness and fear he had adopted during his year of abuse disappeared. He once more took on the mannerisms of the wise old soul that had made him such a wonderful guide dog.

Once Salty was completely secure in his new world, Debbie obtained a harness specifically made for guide dogs. As she approached the collie, he became noticeably excited. Standing as if at attention, he quietly held his position while she put the harness in place and adjusted it. His tail wagging, he waited for her to stand, place her hand on the harness, and give the order to move forward. A smile registered on his graying muzzle as he led Debbie out the door and into the yard. For the next half hour the veteran guide dog showed just how much he loved serving. He nailed every command!

The longer Debbie worked with Salty, the more she considered what it must have been like to go from a service dog to an abused animal. Then another sobering realization left her cold; there were thousands of American military veterans who were homeless. Just like the guide dog, they had served but were now largely forgotten. Perhaps Salty sensed this common bond because as he and Debbie traveled, he seemed drawn to people who called the streets home and to children who were unpopular or disabled.

After being rescued, the collie lived for three happy years. During that time, he charmed hundreds of children at birthday parties, allowed thousands of people who felt displaced to pet his head and feel his acceptance and love, and brought incredible joy into the Abbenante home. And, just because it seemed to bring him so much happiness, Debbie continued to slip on his harness and let Salty guide her around the neighborhood.

When Salty died, he was surrounded by the love of those who deeply appreciated his service, character, and heart. He was also buried with full honors due those who had given so much in service.

Salty's life story is rare in the dog world. Few

service dogs go lacking for a home when they are retired. But in a few cases, guide-dog schools need people to adopt senior dogs. Like Salty, these older canines make incredible additions to a family and also bring a special bonus most other animals cannot. Because of their years of service, they are selfless. On a daily basis, their actions and focus prove the joys, benefits, and blessings of living for others. As the noted missionary doctor Albert Schweitzer once told a group of college students, "I don't know what your destiny will be but I do know the only ones among you who will truly be happy are those who have sought and found how to serve." Salty, and all the other canines and humans who serve, should be put on a pedestal and honored for their gifts of service. They must never be forgotten or thrown away.

FURTHER STORIES OF DEDICATED DOGS

CALLING DOCTOR TRILBY

By John Sherrill

We've heard of physicians making rounds at a hospital. But a dog?

There was one thing dog trainer Jeanne Gurnis wished she could have done for her mother before she died. "Mother was in the intensive care unit, and she kept asking to see Corky, her dog," Jeanne recalled. "But the hospital wouldn't hear of it. All I could bring her were photos. She had me prop the pictures on her nightstand, so Corky would be the first one to greet her when she woke up, just like at home." Still, Jeanne couldn't help wondering how much more her mother's last days could have been brightened if she'd been able to hug her beloved Corky.

So when a local hospital, Westchester Medical Center, just north of New York City, approached her about starting a pet-therapy program—where specially trained animals would visit patients—Jeanne knew she had to give it a try. "This is only a test," the staff warned her. "We'll have to see if pet therapy really does the patients any good."

In the spring of 1999, Jeanne and Trilby, a bright-eyed little corgi who'd been certified through Therapy Dogs International, became the first volunteer pet-therapy team at the hospital. The staff's initial concerns about infection diminished when they learned Trilby had regular checkups and was bathed and groomed before each visit. And resistance melted away entirely as patients' morale and recovery rate improved measurably after Trilby stopped in to see them.

That December a doctor called Trilby to the intensive care unit to see a patient who seemed beyond medical help. Brain-injured in a car accident, Babs Barter had been in a coma for three weeks. Her husband said she loved dogs, so her doctor decided to try Trilby.

Jeanne knew it was a long shot; patients needed to interact with an animal to benefit. As she and Trilby headed into the ICU, Jeanne prayed, as she often did before a tough assignment, *Father, please guide this visit. Thy will be done.*

Babs was on a ventilator, her motionless body bristling with wires and tubes. With the doctor, head nurse and Babs's husband looking on, Jeanne and Trilby went up to her. "Hello, I'm Jeanne Gurnis. I've brought someone to see you."

Jeanne lifted Trilby onto the bed. "I heard you're a dog lover," Jeanne said. No response. She put Babs's limp hand on the dog's back. "Trilby is a Pembroke Welsh corgi. Want to pet her?"

Still no response. Jeanne kept talking. Twenty minutes passed with no hint of awareness from Babs. "You know, if you don't hold Trilby she might fall off the bed." No reaction. Lord, what should I do now? Jeanne wondered.

That's when Trilby took charge. Ever so slowly the little corgi inched closer to Babs's still body. It was a stretch to suppose that a dog—even one as smart as Trilby—understood what Jeanne was getting at. But then Babs's husband exclaimed, "Look…look!"

Jeanne saw it too. Almost imperceptibly, the fingers of the comatose woman moved. "Trilby likes that," Jeanne said to Babs. "Why don't you keep petting her?"

Babs's doctor was so delighted he asked Jeanne and Trilby to come by every day. They did, though Babs's response remained too slight to be sure of.

One morning three weeks after their first visit, Jeanne clearly saw Babs move her fingers. It was unmistakable—she was stroking the dog's soft, thick fur! Two weeks later, Jeanne and Trilby watched Babs's eyes flicker open. When Babs was strong enough to transfer to a rehabilitation center, she got permission for Trilby to visit. Soon Babs was doing so well she was able to go home.

Just before Christmas 2000, a box arrived at Jeanne's house, addressed in a firm, clear hand. "To Trilby Gurnis."

Inside was a huge batch of fresh dog biscuits and a note from Babs Barter. "Baked by me for Trilby, who saved my life. Thanks for the first-class care."

CLONE OF COMFORT DOGS

By Barb Granado

The tragic shootings at Sandy Hook brought all of us together,
including God's most sensitive creatures.

I grabbed the phone on the third ring. I was baby-
sitting my grandkids on a Friday night in mid-
December. All day I'd been so busy I'd never even
switched on the computer. "Hello," I said.

"Have you heard?" It was Sharon, a close friend and
fellow dog handler. Her voice was pinched with strain.
"There's been a shooting at a grade school in Con-
necticut. Twenty first and second graders are dead. I'm
sure we're going to be called to go there, to Newtown.
And, well, I just wanted to talk to you."

My eyes flew to my grandkids, four and two and
a half, sitting contentedly on the couch. Not much
younger than these children who'd been…slaughtered.
Beside them was Hannah, my service dog, specially
trained to give comfort to trauma victims. Sharon
and I both were volunteer handlers. I'd wanted to
be a help to people. But was I ready for such a huge
undertaking? Was Hannah? She was just a puppy,
eleven months old. I'd only had her for a few weeks.
But it was more than that. A handler's job is to stay in

the background, to not show emotion. I looked again at my grandkids. How could I do that when twenty children were dead? Twenty sets of parents facing the worst moment of their lives with virtually the whole nation watching?

I'd have to talk to Tim Hetzner, the director and founder of Comfort Dog Ministry. For years we'd gone to the same Bible study. It was listening to his amazing stories of how the dogs touched the lives of children and adults alike that inspired me to become a handler. Tim had started the program in 2008 after a gunman had killed five people at an Illinois university. He and some other church members had taken their dogs to the campus, hoping to offer compassion in whatever way God led them. He'd found that dogs were able to connect with the students and faculty in a way that no one else could.

"The dogs don't judge," was how Tim explained it at Bible study. "They're patient and loving. And that creates a bond, where people feel safe. We just let the dogs do God's work."

I had known, it wouldn't always be easy. But this was way different. The whole nation was grieving. *Dear God,* I prayed. *If You think I'm not ready, I'll let someone with more experience go instead.*

Tim called soon after Sharon. He told me the team

was ready to go. "The whole town is devastated," he said. "I only wish we had more dogs to send. You can do this, Barb. You just have to step back and let God be in control."

That night in bed I talked to God until sleep finally came. *I don't know how to do this,* I said. *How can I not respond when they're in such pain? I cry too easily. And Hannah. I don't know if she has the patience yet. Maybe if she was older.*

In the morning I woke with an unmistakable feeling: Hannah and I needed to be in Newtown. I thought of those families and how in an instant their lives had been shattered. We couldn't back down. *Okay, God, I'm going,* I thought. I still wasn't sure I had the strength to look into the face of such terrible grief, but I knew I would never find out unless Hannah and I went to Newtown.

Sharon too felt called to go, with her golden retriever, Maggie. "I'll pick you up in an hour," I told Sharon on the phone. It was a fourteen-hour drive, a two-day trip. Two days to think about what was ahead.

I looked at Hannah and wrapped my arms around her. "We can do this," I whispered.

We arrived late Sunday afternoon. Nothing could have prepared us for the scene as we drove into the central business district of Newtown, a quaint picture-postcard New England village. Hundreds of people milled about the town square amid throngs of TV news reporters and camera operators, sending out images to a nation in mourning, to a world in shock. I found a place to park and put Hannah's service vest on her. She seemed to sense that she was about to be tested. Sharon, Maggie, and the rest of the team joined us as we made our way through the crowd. It was freezing cold. But what I noticed more was how quiet it was. No one spoke. It was eerie. You could feel the sorrow and a pervasive sense of despair. It weighed on me. There was nothing to say. Nothing anyone could do to heal the wound.

We reached an opening in the crowd and there in the center was a Christmas tree, lit with colored bulbs. Many in the town had taken down their holiday displays. This lone tree was the town memorial. All around it people had left flowers and teddy bears, photos of the victims, letters, and poems. And a sea of candles. I felt myself coming apart.

I looked into the faces of the people around me, police officers and firefighters. Stunned, shell-shocked, haunted. I wanted so badly to shake their hands, to thank them for their service, to tell them that God was here among us. But I couldn't. All I could do was stand there with Hannah and do nothing. *When would the pain ever lessen?* I wondered. *When would anyone feel comforted? How was that even possible?*

A firefighter came over to us, knelt down, and stroked Hannah's head. "Hey, girl," he whispered. He looked up at me. "Thanks for coming. It means a lot. More than you know." Lines rimmed his eyes; his face was drawn. I couldn't imagine the horror he'd witnessed.

More people noticed us. A small crowd gathered around, everyone wanting to pet the dogs, to talk to them, just wanting to be close to them. Especially children. One little girl wrapped her arms around Hannah and cried into her fur.

Hours later Sharon and I drove back to our hotel room. Neither of us said a word. I was exhausted, drained by the raw emotions. In bed I pressed my face into the pillow. *Dear God,* I prayed. *I don't know if I can do this day after day. Please help me, help me know that You're here. Help Hannah. I am worried this might be too much for her gentle heart.*

The next morning we went to the community center and were ushered to a hallway just inside the door.

It was 7 a.m. and already the building was filled with people. Many were young parents with toddlers and preschoolers. But even the little ones were quiet, staying close to their parents, small hands gripping bigger ones. Their world was suddenly a frightening place. Their innocence stolen from them. No one smiled. Few made eye contact.

I stood there waiting. Hannah sat by me, her eyes riveted on the children, as if she could sense their sadness even from a distance.

A family with a small boy walked slowly up to us. "This is Hannah," I said. "You can pet her. That's why she's here."

The boy looked to his mother, and she nodded. He knelt down next to Hannah and stroked her fur. Barely a trace of emotion. Lips pinched tightly together, as if he were holding the whole world inside. It was heart-wrenching. Even Hannah couldn't reach him.

Hannah moved her great head. She nuzzled the boy's face. All at once he wrapped his arms around her neck. He buried his face in her fur, arms squeezing tight. But Hannah didn't resist even as his tiny hands tugged at her. She seemed to lean in to him.

I bent down to him and whispered, "Hannah really likes secrets. You can tell her anything, and it will be just between you and her."

I couldn't tell at first if he even heard me. And then he raised his lips to her ear and said something. His mouth kept moving, almost silently, until finally his hands relaxed. He patted Hannah on the head. And smiled, just for a second. Not a huge grin. But it was enough.

His parents turned to me. "He's hardly said a word since the shooting," the mother said. "We didn't know what to do. Thank you. Thank you so much."

"I'm glad we could be here," I said. "God bless you." But as they walked away I thought about how little I'd done. Nothing, really. Hannah and God had done all the work.

For a week, Hannah and I ministered to dozens of families and children, police officers and firefighters. A week of moments shared by a dog and a person who was struggling to find hope in a senseless act of mass murder. Too soon we had to leave. We left a community still deep in sorrow, with many difficult days ahead. But they weren't alone. Far from it. Together we'd see each other through even this. In the presence of our greatest pain there is always one great healing power that reaches us in profound and unexpected ways. On the way back to Chicago, Hannah and Maggie settled in comfortably. They slept almost all the way home.

DOG TO THE RESCUE

By Deby Duzan

She lost interest in everything. Even in the pets she'd always loved.

Summer was coming, and I knew that was bad.
My seventeen-year-old daughter, Seleta, hated the
summertime. To her summer meant nothing to do,
and that meant boredom, which only aggravated her
depressive tendencies.

We'd become aware of the problem when she
was just ten. She lost interest in everything—school,
friends. She didn't even enjoy playing with animals
anymore.

It wasn't like her at all. Though at first I chalked it
up to growing pains, when she didn't pull out of her
funk I began to think it was something more serious.
I took her to the doctor. Seleta was diagnosed with
depression. Finally we knew what was wrong, but that
didn't solve the problem. Seleta was still in so much
pain, and it hurt me to see her like that. I wanted to
make it all go away, have everything be fine again.

Over the next seven years, I learned that as much
as I wanted to cure Seleta, I couldn't. We had some
rocky times. As she entered her teens, I wondered if she
would ever regain some kind of balance. Seleta hated

taking her medication. She said it didn't help, and she didn't like that one of the side effects was weight gain. Kids at school would make fun of her, and she'd stop taking her medication. But the weight stayed on, yet another thing to be depressed about. Then school would let out, summer would come and Seleta would be more depressed than ever. It was a vicious cycle.

When Seleta was down, she wanted nothing other than to sleep. It seemed to be all she ever did. All day, every day. *Lord,* I'd pray, *please help Seleta to feel better.* There's got to be some way to make her happy again. I talked to her all the time, trying to find out how she was doing every day. I took her shopping with me and made sure we kept up our weekly night out together. I knew that a trip to the market or a dinner and a movie would force Seleta to get out of the house. It couldn't hurt, I figured, and it might even help. I wouldn't give up on my daughter.

Seleta did have good days, even good weeks or months. But inevitably, as the dark cloud closed in on her once again, she'd slowly sink back into a deep funk. The worst of it came in 1999, right in the middle of her junior year in high school. Three times, Seleta's depression got so bad that she had to check into a behavioral health center, once because of a suicide attempt. I prayed harder than ever, and so did our family and friends.

Eventually her condition stabilized, and she managed to do well in her classes despite the disruptions. But as the semester drew to a close I worried. Would the long summer ahead drag Seleta back down? I was hopeful when she announced she was determined to get a job, just to have something to do, some reason to get out of bed every day.

Seleta found work at a local pet superstore, and started when school let out for the year. Right away she loved her job, and soon I could tell a remarkable change was taking place in my daughter. "I get to talk to lots of different people," she would tell me after work. "And there's all kinds of dogs to pet." Seleta had always loved animals—especially dogs, the bigger the better. Now she was talking about a school in Denver, where she wanted to go after graduation to study to become a veterinary technician. I worried how she'd manage on her own so far from home. Still, I was relieved she seemed to be less gloomy.

One day Seleta called me from the store. "Mom," she said, "I just saw the best dog! She's a big old English mastiff, and she's so beautiful! The dog-rescue lady from next door brought her into the store today. She needs a permanent home. Can I take her?"

"Your dad won't be too happy," I said, thinking of our two cats and the Great Dane named Onyx that

Seleta had convinced me to adopt, supposedly as a birthday gift for her father.

"Please, Mom? At least come see her."

I went down to the pet store, and there I met Maya. "Isn't she beautiful, Mom?" Seleta said.

That thing? She was gigantic, almost as big as our Great Dane. Plus, she drooled. But when I looked away from the dog and back at my daughter, I saw she was beaming, in a way I hadn't seen in a long, long time. *Well, Seleta does want to go away to school,* I convinced myself. A dog would be a good companion, and one that big certainly would be protection for a young woman living on her own.

"OK," I agreed. "But only if when you go away to Denver, she goes along with you." We paid the thirty-dollar adoption fee and took the dog to our vet, Phil Trokey; he'd been taking care of our pets for years. "Maya's in excellent health," he assured us after the exam. So we brought her home for good.

Seleta enrolled Maya in an obedience class where she sailed through with flying colors. "She's better than all the other dogs, Mom," Seleta told me. "She does almost everything she's supposed to do when she's told to do it." Seleta would come home from class and show us the latest command Maya had learned to obey. She was so excited that for the first time in a long while, I allowed myself to feel a bit of hope. The same girl who once could barely drag herself out of bed was now doing something that made her feel good. I prayed it would last.

One day, in the waiting room at the vet's, a little boy came over to Maya and started petting her. She was very gentle, as always, and even seemed careful not to drool on the little fellow. Not that he would have minded. He was delighted with the giant dog. "I don't know why I didn't think of this before," Phil said. "Maya is good with people. You might want to look into her becoming a therapy dog."

A big smile appeared on Seleta's face as soon as Phil spoke those words. She found a trainer and started working to get Maya ready for the tests she'd need to pass to be certified as a therapy dog. Meanwhile, the summer I'd worried so much about was coming to a close. Seleta pulled through it just fine. When school started she managed to juggle schoolwork and the training classes with Maya.

Seleta called the behavioral health center where she'd been a patient and asked if they'd be interested in a therapy dog. She was told to bring Maya in for an interview. The staff loved the dog so much that they said they'd be glad to have her and Seleta come in twice a week after she got her certification. When she heard that, it was like she came back to life all at once.

Training Maya for therapy had become therapy in itself. Now when Seleta took Maya out for walks she would introduce the dog to anyone they came across. One day she went over to the grounds of the elementary school next to our house. A few of the teachers fell immediately in love with Maya. "You know," said one of them, "Maya looks just like Mudge."

"Who?"

"It's a dog in a children's book series. A boy named Henry gets a huge dog named Mudge, and they become the best of friends. My students love those books. Say," she went on, "why don't you come to my class with Maya one day and read one of the books to the class. They'd love it!"

Seleta went, and the kids did love it. Soon after that, we visited my grandmother, who lives in a nursing home. Maya came along to meet Seleta's great-grandmother and all the other residents of the home. One elderly woman who sat with a stuffed puppy in her arms took a real liking to Maya. Seleta spent a long time with the woman, and they both talked about their dogs. At the end of the visit, both the woman and my daughter looked happy. Already, even before getting her certification, Maya was a success at pet therapy.

I'm not saying that Seleta's depression just vanished overnight. But somehow, working with Maya made it easier for Seleta to cope. Eventually she got engaged with the world and with people again. Maya made her want to. And that helped her maintain a balance. I took it in stride when Seleta announced that she wanted to be a foster parent for other rescued mastiffs. But I was floored when we started doing some research. The average adoption fee for an abandoned mastiff was three-hundred and fifty dollars. It seemed a bit steep, especially since almost all those abandoned dogs were in poor shape, with severe health problems or some kind of disfigurement.

I thought of Maya. She had been in perfect health, and she was as gentle as a lamb. Why would someone have abandoned her? A mastiff puppy in good shape could cost as much as fifteen hundred dollars. There was no way we would have been able to afford that. Yet our adoption fee was a mere thirty dollars.

How and why had it all happened? Well, I know Maya's a dog, but to me she's also kind of an angel. She came as an answer to prayer, didn't she?

Maya got her certification as a therapy dog, and now when she and Seleta leave the house to head for the nursing home, I see how content my daughter is. She's doing work that means something, giving of herself to people in need.

I thank God every day for the giant, drooling dog who has been my daughter's guide to life.

JACK, THERAPY DOG

By Diana Aydin

Happiness is a warm puppy, especially in this retirement community.

He was the runt of the breeder's litter. That's the first thing Laura Diachenko noticed about the black-and-white miniature Australian Shepherd. Unlike the other puppies, this one wasn't squirmy. He clung to her when she picked him up.

Could he be the one? she wondered. She'd only visited the breeder on a whim.

No. No way. He wasn't the right breed for starters. Laura wanted a big dog—specifically, a Bernese Mountain Dog—that she could train to be a therapy animal. It had been her dream for twenty-two years, ever since she'd been laid up for a week in the hospital recovering from back surgery. The one highlight had been the visit she received from a Bernese Mountain therapy dog.

Now a senior living counselor at Gulf Coast Village, a Volunteers of America–sponsored retirement community in Cape Coral, Florida, Laura felt her dream could become a reality. She had read up on the benefits a therapy dog could offer seniors dealing with illness and dementia, and she had gotten approval to start a daily therapy dog program at Gulf Coast Village.

This runt was nothing like the dog she'd had in mind. But there was something about him. His mismatched eyes, one black and one brown. And the way he nuzzled his way into her arms, grunting in pleasure. The breeder turned to his wife and said, "That's her dog." Laura couldn't help but agree. "I'll take him," she said.

Laura took the puppy home, naming him Jack. Shortly after his first birthday, he completed his training through the Alliance of Therapy Dogs and was ready to go to work. There was only one problem. Because Laura worked full-time, she couldn't supervise his visits with residents at Gulf Coast Village during the day. No one else on staff could do it either. Who else was there?

One person popped into Laura's head—Roger Wieland. A ninety-year-old retired veterinarian and World War II vet, he'd been living at Gulf Coast Village with his wife, Irene, for the past three years. Before moving to Florida, Roger had owned three veterinary hospitals in Michigan. When Jack was a puppy, Laura had introduced him to Roger. They'd clicked right away.

"Would you be Jack's handler here?" Laura asked Roger.

"Me?" he said. "I'm no spring chicken!"

Laura assured Roger that he could keep his normal schedule of activities but add visits to Gulf Coast Village's assisted living residents. Roger's eyes lit up. "I'll do it," he said.

That's how Roger and Jack became the most recognizable duo at Gulf Coast Village. Their day starts promptly at 8 a.m., when Roger stops by Laura's office to pick Jack up. First stop: tai chi class. Jack gets up to greet every person who enters the classroom and waits patiently as Roger exercises. The rest of the day is spent meeting and greeting residents, including people in the memory care and rehabilitation units. "To see them together is remarkable," Laura says. "Jack looks at Roger like Opie looks up at his dad on *The Andy Griffith Show*."

Tom Hafer, a Volunteers of America minister and chaplain at Gulf Coast Village, says he's never seen a dog quite like Jack. Not only does he get residents up and moving, but he's able to step into the world of people with Alzheimer's and dementia.

"He allows residents to live in the present," Tom says. "In that moment, aches and pains are suspended. Jack has an uncanny ability to sense when someone needs him."

Like when Roger took a tumble in the hallway last year. Nothing was broken. Even so, Jack never left

Roger's side. "Jack was continuously licking him as if to heal him," Laura says. "I didn't train him to do any of that. He's just a very old soul."

That old soul has made Jack an invaluable member of the Gulf Coast Village community. Residents and staff greet him like he's a rock star. Not bad for the runt of the litter.

"A dog will light up people in a different way," Tom says. "Jack is very much a minister to us all."

SOME SERVICE DOG

By Brenda Mosley

I thought Toby would make a good companion dog, the kind of helper dog Farley had been. Toby, though, he wasn't even good.

Something poked me in the face. Something cold and wet. "Not again, Toby," I moaned groggily, pushing my dog's nose away from mine. I rolled over. Just as I was falling asleep again, he nipped at my sleeve. "Toby, stop!" I commanded. He flopped down next to my bed and promptly started snoring. I didn't even care about the noise. Maybe I'd finally be able to get some sleep myself. I drifted off.

A tug on my foot. *What now?* I forced my eyes open. Toby was trying to pull off my sock. I nudged him away, glaring at him. He cocked his head and looked at me quizzically. My alarm clock hadn't gone off yet. It was only 5:00 a.m. I'd been planning to get up early for my doctor's appointment, but not this early. Would this dog ever learn?

Every night for weeks now he'd been waking me up. Not just once or twice. Constantly. I couldn't remember the last time I got a good night's rest. And, Lord knows, I needed it. Living with both cerebral palsy and multiple sclerosis was debilitating. If my old service dog were still around, I might have coped, but Toby? All I'd been able to train him to do so far was fetch my slippers. Some service dog! I needed help with a lot more than that.

My old dog, a retriever named Farley, had only taken basic obedience lessons when he came to live with me. I'd never trained a dog before, but he was so smart it didn't take long for me to teach him to do all kinds of things around the house. Farley would bring me the phone, get a can of soda from the fridge, and take clothes out of the dryer. He carried grocery sacks, helped me up from chairs, and steadied me if my walk got wobbly. He even pulled me in a wheelchair those times I had to use one.

For ten years he was my companion, my partner. Together we helped other people with disabilities train their service dogs. Thanks to Farley, I'd been able to avoid the fate I dreaded—moving into an assisted-living center—even after my condition deteriorated so much that I had to quit my job teaching preschool and go on disability. He was a real answer to prayer, my Farley. A champion service dog.

I was inconsolable when he died. What dog could ever replace him? But I knew that if I wanted to continue living on my own, I'd have to get a new service dog. So I went to a kennel, hoping I would find another answer to prayer. Yet even I couldn't quite believe the retriever I spotted in an outdoor run. *He looks just like Farley!* Long legs, reddish fur and all. Toby was his name, the kennel owner said.

I took Toby for a test walk on a gravel path, a tricky surface for me. He walked beside me slowly and deliberately, seeming to sense my hesitation. *Good temperament*, I thought. The only drawback: Ideally, a service dog is fully trained by age two, and Toby was already four.

But Toby's uncanny resemblance to Farley...what else could he be but another answer to prayer? *I bet I can teach him to act like Farley too,* I thought. I had a good track record when it came to training service dogs.

I brought Toby home. The first thing he did was tear through every room in the house. "Stop!" I ordered. He paused, looked at me, then bolted through the doggy door to the backyard.

Toby had been kenneled outdoors his whole life. It would take time for him to adjust to living in my house. I just didn't expect it to take this long. Everything scared him. When the phone rang, he howled and cowered in a corner. When the dryer buzzed, he ran for cover. When the deliveryman knocked on the door, Toby jumped a mile high, barking frantically.

Toby's sole talent seemed to be napping. He would
drop off right in the middle of a training session. Once
I spent an entire morning rolling a tennis ball across
the floor. "Fetch," I said. Sometimes Toby grabbed the
tennis ball in his mouth, but he wouldn't bring it back
to me. *Aren't retrievers bred to do this?* I decided to try
something softer. Maybe it would be easier for him.

I dropped one of my fuzzy slippers near him. "Get
the slipper, Toby." Toby ignored the slipper, walked
over to me, put his head on my leg and yawned. "Off," I
said, pushing his head gently toward the floor. "Get the
slipper." Toby curled up at my feet and dozed off.

Something in me just snapped. "Toby," I called.
Loudly. He jolted awake and looked at me. I bent
down. "This is a slipper!" I yelled. I pushed it into his
mouth. "How could I have ever thought you were an
answer to prayer!" I got up, stumbled into the bath-
room, and slammed the door.

I stared at my reflection in the mirror. I looked
drained. The MS was making me weaker and weaker.
Dogs don't respond well to anger, I reminded myself.
*You've got to try again with Toby. You don't have the
strength to start over with another dog.*

I opened the door. Toby sat in the exact spot I'd
left him. His tail wagged. He still had the slipper in his
mouth. I didn't know whether to laugh or cry. "Drop," I

said. Right away he did. "Good dog!" I patted his head. He spent the rest of the day happily retrieving my slipper.

But that was all he learned in two months of training. I couldn't count on Toby day-to-day. Certainly not in an emergency. I couldn't count on him for anything, really, except waking me up practically every night.

And I've had enough of that, I thought, swinging my legs over the edge of my bed and sitting up. I eyed my so-called service dog. Toby sprawled on the floor, apparently satisfied that he'd successfully kept me from yet another night's rest. *Lord, You couldn't have meant this dog for me.*

I stuck my feet into my slippers and stood. Might as well get ready for my doctor's appointment. Prepare myself to tell her I'd made the decision I had dreaded my whole adult life. I was going to give up my dog, my house, my independence. Could she help me find a place in an assisted-living center?

Later that morning my doctor ushered me into her examination room. "Are you okay, Brenda?" She said with concern. "You look tired."

"That's because I'm not sleeping."

"Why not?" she asked.

I told her about my problems with Toby. "Maybe he's just acting out because I've been working him so hard," I said. "But I wouldn't have to if he'd just learn."

My doctor listened to my lungs, then checked my nose and throat. "It might be good that Toby's been waking you."

"Good?"

"You're showing signs of sleep apnea. People with this condition stop breathing during the night. Left untreated, it could lead to a heart attack or stroke." She set up an appointment for me at a sleep clinic the following week.

Toby and I went to the clinic together. They said it was OK since he was a service dog. My bedroom for the night was connected to a control room, where observers would monitor me while I slept. Normally that would've bothered me. But I was too tired to care. A nurse attached electrodes to my head, chest, and legs. I stretched out on the bed, and Toby curled up on the floor beside me. As usual, he conked out right away. Well before I did.

And as usual, Toby barely let me sleep a wink. He'd get up to lick my hands and snort in my face. *He's hopeless. Incorrigible*, I thought. At least now my doctor will know what I'm up against.

I took Toby with me to get the sleep-test results. "Looks like my suspicion was on target, Brenda," my doctor said. "You stopped breathing fifteen times during the night. Your dog woke you every time."

Just like that, everything came into focus. *No wonder poor Toby naps so much*, I thought. He's worn out from trying to save my life! He was like those dogs I'd read about who have a remarkable talent. They can sense when a seizure or a cardiac episode is about to hit their owners and alert them.

I looked at Toby, dozing beside my chair. I leaned over and stroked the soft reddish fur behind one of his ears. He opened his eyes and started to his feet. "No, you rest, Toby, you've earned it," I told him. "Will you give me another chance? I'll be as patient with you as you've been with me, I promise."

Toby licked my hand and lay down.

My doctor outfitted me with an oxygen tube to regulate my breathing while I sleep. Now Toby wakes me only if the tube slips off. It's pretty amazing how well we learned to work together once we both got enough rest. Before long, Toby could do everything Farley had done. These days Toby and I train other dogs to help people with disabilities. He loves to demonstrate how to get a can of soda from the fridge, carry a bag and, of course, fetch slippers. My Toby is some service dog, all right. A real answer to prayer, one I didn't even know I needed, yet I couldn't live without.

TRUSTED PARTNER

By Penney Gillett Silvius

When a client started to cry, Francine became a therapist.

Sometimes God answers our prayers in ways we could never imagine. He did this in my work as a marriage, family, and child counselor. I am confined to a wheelchair because of multiple sclerosis, but I had always felt my disability helped me in my work. I could identify with people's problems and gain greater insight into their needs.

The time came, however, when I needed more physical help, God answered my many prayers through the form of a beautiful golden retriever named Francine. In 1988 Francine came to me from Canine Companions for Independence, in Santa Rosa, California, a group that trains dogs to assist people with disabilities, including service dogs for the mobility-impaired and hearing dogs for the hard of hearing.

Francine had a cheerful, loving personality. She picked up items I dropped, turned on light switches, opened doors by pulling on a tie attached to the handle, helped me balance when I got into bed, and even pulled my wheelchair. We were alike in many ways: Both of us were strawberry-blond, we both adored my husband and, most surprisingly, I discovered we shared the same professional tendencies.

When my clients arrived, Francine and I met them at the door. After brief greetings I sent Francine back to her spot under my desk and the client and I began work. At first I wondered what my clients would think when they saw a dog lying under my desk. I prayed that Francine would not be a distraction and that she would remain quietly unobtrusive. But God had other plans for her.

My first clue to Francine's value came when I noticed she could help me assess a client's emotional state. For instance, if someone was trying to avoid talking about something painful, he or she usually spent time interacting with Francine until I could draw the person out.

But I was not prepared for what Francine did when a client started to cry. As one woman began to disclose her problems, she broke down in tears and could not continue talking. Francine stirred at my feet and looked up at me. Something told me what she wanted to do was right, so I nodded. She rose, padded over to the woman, placed her chin on her lap and looked up as if she really understood. As the woman reached down and stroked Francine's head, her sobs subsided. She wiped her eyes and said, "I think I can talk about things better now."

We had a good session. After the woman left, I thanked Francine and told her, "Looks like we're going to be working together from now on."

I don't know what I would have done without her in a session with Sally*—a woman who was bitter, depressed, and full of despair. Sally had become antisocial, reclusive, and was ready to give up living. I too was feeling hopeless, for we weren't making much progress.

Then, knowing how much joy Francine brought me, I thought perhaps she could bring some to Sally. At my command she went over to Sally and put her front paws on her lap. Sally leaned down and began petting her, then hugging her. As she did, her expression softened and her eyes brightened. It was a turning point. We began making real progress in Sally's therapy, and her life took on a new direction.

George* presented a different obstacle. Very reserved, he spoke so slowly that it took him a long time to express himself. We could barely identify his dilemma before his time was up. One day Francine wandered from her spot and lay at George's feet. As he began stroking her, he started to speak more fluently. From then on Francine was at George's feet whenever he was present, and George was able to articulate his concerns.

Perhaps Francine's greatest hour came during a child's devastating trauma. Four-year-old Amy* had been sexually molested. Deeply upset by the abuse, she was further overwhelmed when she told her mother, who immediately became hysterical. As a result of her mother's reaction, Amy refused to talk to anyone about what had happened to her. Because I knew the family from church, the pastor recommended Amy's parents bring her to me.

Since Amy already knew Francine, I took both of them into our children's room, where I conduct play therapy, while Amy's parents waited in my office. I stayed to one side while Amy and Francine sat together on the floor. As Amy petted Francine, she began telling the dog what had happened. Francine "listened" intently, and so did I. As a result, I was able to help Amy and her parents begin to heal.

Over and over, I have thanked the Lord for Francine. When I prayed for a canine companion, I did not know God would also send me a cotherapist, a partner in my practice.

*All clients' names have been changed.

WHEN MICHAEL MET ROSIE

By Claire Guthrie

My older kids wanted a dog. But I worried about my youngest. He couldn't tell me what he wanted.

W e're getting a dog! We're getting a dog!" the kids chanted from the back of our car on the way to Pennsylvania to pick up Rosie, our new Lab, from her foster home. I glanced back at my teenager, Aaron, his younger sister, Rachael, seven, and brother Joshua, five, who hadn't stopped talking about Rosie since we'd pulled out of our driveway in Virginia an hour before. Only my two-year-old, Michael, was silent. He was just as excited, but he couldn't join in with the chatter of his siblings. I felt a familiar ache in my chest, knowing how badly Michael wanted to join in and knowing it was impossible. It was a pain I felt often, ever since we found out about Michael's condition.

I knew something was different about Michael at six months old. Josh and Rachael walked and talked early. But our otherwise healthy-looking baby boy had trouble even crawling; Michael couldn't roll over and he couldn't sit up without toppling. Even more troubling, he never developed baby talk. I wondered if he'd ever speak. His brother Aaron has cerebral palsy, and

I feared Michael might have a disability too. In fact, Michael was diagnosed with dyspraxia, a developmental disorder that makes it difficult to perform complex movements. Michael's trouble with speaking was part of that disorder, called Childhood Apraxia of Speech. He wanted to speak, but his mind just wouldn't let him.

Even now, at two years and three months, he still couldn't say much more than "mama" or "dada" when he wanted us for something. And often, we couldn't understand what he wanted. His speech therapist helped us teach him some basic sign language. Even that was hard for him. A few days earlier, Michael tried to ask me for something, but he couldn't form the signs. Instead, he began gesturing wildly. "I'm sorry, Michael. I don't understand," I told him. His face turned a deep shade of red; he went into a tantrum, letting out a high-pitched scream. I felt so helpless. My baby was hurting—and I couldn't do anything for him.

I looked in the rearview mirror back at Michael, who was staring out the window. This dog, I hoped, would be something he could enjoy. My husband, Doug, and I had done our research. We looked for a Labrador, a breed known to be good with kids. A young dog, so it could grow up with our children. We found Rosie on the website for a Lab rescue agency.

A fourteen-month-old chocolate Lab with experience around babies, children, and cats. All of our "dream dog" qualities. But would she be right for our family? Was I wrong to hope? Finally we pulled up to Rosie's foster home. I silently prayed, *Please, God, let Rosie be right for our kids…especially Michael, but don't let me hope for too much.*

Doug lifted Michael out of his car seat while I went to the door with the other kids. "You must be here to see Rosie," the woman said. And there Rosie was, standing in the foyer, tongue hanging out, her tail wagging wildly. Aaron, Rachael, and Joshua ran up to her. "Rosie, you're so beautiful," Rachael said, ruffling her smooth fur.

"Hi, Rosie," said Aaron, scratching her behind the ears.

Love at first sight, I thought. But what about my two-year-old? Michael ambled over. He patted her gently on the head. Rosie nuzzled against him. I breathed a sigh of relief.

I was about to follow the woman into the other room to talk to her about the dog when I heard a voice, an unfamiliar voice. "Rosie," the voice said, strong and clear. "Rosie!" It was Michael. I looked at Doug, my mouth agape. "Rosie!" he said again, nuzzling against the dog. Now, Doug and I were the speechless ones.

Rosie sat in the back with the kids on the way home. "You're going to love our house, Rosie Pops," I said.

The kids loved the nickname. The whole ride back, that's what we called her. We were about halfway home when Michael spoke again. "Rosie Pops," he said. One word was amazing enough, but two words together? In one day? Doug and I chalked it up to Michael's excitement. *Don't get your hopes up*, I reminded myself. How often had I seen progress when there was none? *God, I prayed once more, make this dog a good fit for our family.*

A few days later I was folding laundry, watching the kids play with Rosie. Michael stood next to her, petting her as she rubbed up against him. Then, without warning, she jumped, and Michael lost his balance. I watched in horror as he fell over. I dropped everything and rushed to him. But I calmed down when I saw Michael laughing. He pushed off the carpet and stood, following Rosie again as she raced around the room. I watched more closely. Rosie wasn't being reckless. Every time she nudged Michael, she did it gently, almost as if she were testing him. And each time he fell, she waited by his side, studying him until he rose to his feet. It was a little game they were playing. A game Rosie was using to learn things about Michael.

The next night, at dinner, Michael shocked everyone when he said "juice." Right out of the blue! A day later, he said "dog." It's hard to describe the astonishment that took over our house. Over the next few weeks, he added more words: candy, cookie, car. He was also becoming less clumsy—rarely stumbling. His speech therapist was baffled. "Kids with apraxia don't progress like this," she told me.

I was baffled too. I went on an apraxia website and emailed for information. "Is there anything about dogs helping kids with apraxia?" I asked. Yes, as it turned out. Studies found the stimulation a dog brings can awaken muscles necessary for speech and other bodily movements. Each time Michael laughed, fell, and got back up again, his brain was busily connecting the dots between his muscles and his actions. Now I knew why he was improving.

I went up to tuck Michael into bed. He was exhausted from playing with Rosie all day. I pulled the blanket up to his chest and gave him a kiss. Michael moved his lips. "Luv vu," he said. *Did he say that?* Michael spoke again. "Luv vu," he said.

I wrapped my arms around him. "I love you, Michael," I whispered through my tears. "I love you too." I shut off his light and headed to the living room. Rosie lay curled up by the TV. I stroked behind her ears and told her what a good girl she was. She was teaching Michael so much—and me as well. God answers prayers in many ways. This time He chose a dog to answer ours. Hope comes in many forms, and I must never forsake it.

WONDER DOG

By Linda Rae Smith

I had to quit the job I loved after I got sick. I thought everything was over. Then I met Tucson.

It started with small things. I'd wake up in the morning feeling weak and unrested, despite having slept through the night. Maneuvering the groceries out of my car, I'd suddenly get so dizzy I'd have to put the bag down on the ground to get my bearings again. As someone who has lived with MS for more than thirty years, I was used to coping with my symptoms. But these new episodes were distressing.

I taught elementary-age kids who had mental and physical challenges. I know what it means to struggle with tasks that others do without a thought. Helping people succeed at something they had to struggle for gave me considerable satisfaction. "But they who wait for the Lord shall renew their strength, they shall mount up with wings like eagles, they shall run and not be weary, they shall walk and not faint." Those lines from Isaiah were the cornerstone of my life.

I had always believed that my work with kids was the reason the good Lord put me on this earth. And just as I helped those kids, so God would help me. He had walked every step of the way with me through my illness, and I knew he would continue to do so.

But for once, I'd underestimated my MS. I slurred my words so badly that the kids sometimes couldn't understand what I said. My legs felt shaky and uncertain, as if they might give way at any moment.

Then a group of fifth-graders rushed past me in the hallway heading to the lunchroom one day at noon. I reeled and caught myself at the last second before going down. It wasn't the first time, but it was the worst. The incident shook me up so much that I was no good for the rest of the day.

I'd always taught part-time, for the pure joy of it. My husband, Don's, income kept our household going. Now I wondered if I could go on. One morning in class, dizzy and exhausted though the day had hardly begun, I looked at the roomful of kids in front of me. Kids with problems of their own—kids who needed more help than I could give them. I could barely get up from behind my desk. Help them? Who was I kidding? *Lord, I can't do this anymore.* These kids deserve more. That week I applied for disability retirement.

I did my best to stay active. I forced myself to get up in the morning whether I had anything scheduled for the day or not. I forced myself to get out of bed no matter how bad I felt. But there were days I felt so bad I could barely pray.

One afternoon, I looked out the window and saw Ritchie, the ten-year-old from a few doors down, playing with a toy truck on the sidewalk. He looked so small, crouched there under the big Colorado sky. Lonely. Kind of the way I felt. *Lord, I know You still have a purpose for me. Help me find a way out of this.*

"Why don't you get a dog?" Don suggested that night at dinner. "There are all kinds of service dogs these days. Not just seeing eye dogs. A good dog— maybe a golden retriever—could help you get around, keep you steady on your feet. You need a helper. A service dog."

A dog? Was he serious? Was that what it had come to? I got on the internet. Don was right. Golden retrievers could be trained to do just about anything. All they wanted in return was love and support. Not much different than people, really. I found a breeder nearby. Don and I brought home a beautiful seven-week-old puppy that we named Tucson. I had never seen such an abundance of life in such a small, furry bundle. The embodiment of joy, energy, and love. Pure, devoted love. Our vet put us in touch with an excellent dog trainer. Ever hear of the movie called *The Natural?* That was Tucson. A flat-out natural. "He's a people dog," the breeder had said. She wasn't kidding. He caught on faster than I did.

Tucson's main job was to act as my "stabilizer." He wore a harness that I held onto as I walked. If I felt weak or wobbly, I'd lean into his strong body. Tucson knew exactly what to do—steady me.

Everyday activities that had become more difficult— walks around the neighborhood, trips to the grocery— were suddenly in reach again. Service dogs can't be petted while they're working because it distracts them, but everyone stopped to admire Tucson. Sometimes he'd get a little distracted by all the praise. I couldn't blame him. It felt pretty good to me too. I felt full of new energy and enthusiasm. I had my old life back!

Almost. I was still lonely without my kids. *But that's all over*, I chided myself.

One afternoon there was a knock at the door. Tucson trotted over to see who was there. It was Ritchie, the boy from down the street.

"Mrs. Smith, if Tucson's off duty, can he play with me?"

I looked down at Tucson. Well? he seemed to say.

"Sure, Ritchie. Why don't you two go around back?"

Tucson darted out the door and led the way. I peeked through the curtain and watched them play fetch all afternoon. Finally I had to call Tucson in for supper. "Thanks, Mrs. Smith. Thanks, Tucson," Ritchie said. "What a great dog!"

Tucson inhaled his food, drained his water bowl, and stretched out on his bed with a mighty groan of contentment. I went over and stroked his head. "I'm not the only one around here who loves kids, am I?" The strangest feeling came over me. Tucson looked up at me with his kind dark eyes, almost as if saying, Don't you get it?

Those words of Isaiah's came to me again. *Lord, I think I get it.* I called Tucson's vet and asked if she knew of any service organizations Tucson and I could volunteer for. She suggested Denver Pet Partners, our local chapter of the Delta Society, an organization that works to enhance the lives of all kinds of people through contact with service animals.

Tucson and I went back into training—six weeks' worth. Soon after, we visited our first kids at a special-needs program in an elementary school. That first morning I walked through the front doors with Tucson. The one-of-a-kind smell that schools always seem to have unleashed a flood of emotion. I felt Tucson next to me. Don't worry, that pressure told me. I'm here for you.

We found our classroom. Most of the kids were in wheelchairs. A boy of about eight sat off from the rest of the group. Tucson padded over. The boy looked at the teacher and me, his eyes holding an equal measure of fear and excitement.

"It's OK," I said. "Take hold of his harness." The boy grabbed it, stood up, and took a few halting steps forward. Tucson walked slowly and steadily, keeping pace with him. The boy stopped. Tucson looked up. It was a look of encouragement. Don't worry, I'll help you, he seemed to say. The boy took a couple more steps, each more confident than the last. "You can do it!" I cheered. I could just see the confidence flooding through him. I knew how that felt.

Tucson and I visit classrooms on a regular basis. I'd say it's a toss-up who enjoys this work more: the kids, Tucson, or me. In addition to his school assignments, Tucson often goes to church with me. He has proudly served as both Christmas dog—carrying a basket of toys—and Easter dog. One year, the pastor asked the kids what happens on Easter. A little girl raised her hand and announced, "The Easter puppy comes."

Of course there are plenty of things I need help with that Tucson can't do. He can't open an extra-tight lid on a jar of mayonnaise, and he can't make my voice more clear when I slur my words. In a way, though, he does make those things easier to deal with, simply by his presence—a presence that lets me know God is always close by too. Those words of Isaiah's are as true for me now as they ever were before. For only God could use a golden retriever to show how great His care can be.

A NOTE FROM THE EDITORS

We hope you enjoyed *Service Tails: More Stories of Man's Best Hero* by Ace Collins, published by the Books and Inspirational Media Division of Guideposts, a nonprofit organization that touches millions of lives every day through products and services that inspire, encourage, help you grow in your faith, and celebrate God's love.

Thank you for making a difference with your purchase of this book, which helps fund our many outreach programs to military personnel, prisons, hospitals, nursing homes, and educational institutions.

We also create many useful and uplifting online resources. Visit Guideposts.org to read true stories of hope and inspiration, access OurPrayer network, sign up for free newsletters, download free e-books, join our Facebook community, and follow our stimulating blogs.

To learn about other Guideposts publications, including the best-selling devotional *Daily Guideposts*, go to Guideposts.org/Shop, call (800) 932-2145, or write to Guideposts, PO Box 5815, Harlan, Iowa 51593.